The Lobbyist

• • •

Part One

John O. Murphy Ed.D.

ISBN: 150022278X
ISBN 13: 9781500222789
Library of Congress Control Number: 2014912288
CreateSpace Independent Publishing Platform
North Charleston, South Carolina

To my wife, Karen

Lobbying is a simple job. Visit a man nine times and don't ask for anything. On your tenth visit, ask, and you will get whatever you want.
—John O. Murphy Jr., Ed.D

Disclaimer

This book is a work of fiction. Resemblance to any living or dead person or actual events is merely and simply coincidental. Names, people, companies, associations, groups, locations, and dealings are fictional and created by the author's inventiveness and imagination.

Table of Contents

SECTION I

A NEW LIFE IN STATE POLITICS

CHAPTER 1

BULLSHITTING THE BULLSHITTERS

INTRODUCTION

Two good ole boys, Mike and James, worked in jobs from eight to five like most people in America, and they met routinely two or three afternoons each week after work.

On this particular rainy day, Mike and James ducked into a rather notorious bar located near the state capitol that was frequented by politicos and "loose" women. They went there to have their daily cocktail and to listen to each other complain about his job. Little did Mike and James know it, but their lives were going to change—that is, change forever. Not only from their fed-up attitude toward working for someone else, but from what they were about to overhear and observe in the bar that afternoon. Mike and James would never complain about their jobs again.

James and Mike didn't know it yet, but they were on their way to careers as independent lobbyists—a job few people have ever experienced. They were going to enter a field of work in which less than 1 percent of the population has the opportunity to experience. As in all lines of work, there's the good, the bad, and the ugly—and a lobbyist can be one, two, or all three. If you're a lobbyist, the public mostly believes you're a crook, you're on the take, and you're scheming against the public interest. Most lobbyists are simply guilty by association. They work in the arena of law dominated by many politicians and individuals who are only interested in self-enrichment, getting laid, and holding on to power. James and Mike were about to associate with the power brokers of society that many men and women only wish they could understand, much less get to know and work with daily. They would soon learn that life in politics is not what they expected.

THE GOOD OLE BOYS

James was a good-looking man with a radio voice and for a short time was a television weather reporter. He was the spitting image of Robert Redford, a handsome and beautiful man by anyone's standards. Women were always after him, but he prided himself in being very selective of the women with whom he associated.

James grew up in a broken home where cursing and fighting were common. He became very street-smart, to the point that it often got him into trouble—that is, socially into trouble, not anything offensive to society like breaking the law. James made it through four years of college at one of the state's regional universities with a degree in journalism and a minor in political science. He held several jobs, including teaching social studies in his younger years at a large high school in the suburbs. He was an excellent teacher and liked his students. For a short period, he had worked for a government agency. James was thirty-five, but looked young for his age. He enjoyed playing the stock market, where he has been on both the winning and losing sides. He won more often than he lost.

Since James had a charismatic personality, everyone liked him. He looked people in the eye, and they always believed that he was interested in whatever they were talking about, whether he was or not. Because of his good looks and the way he carried himself when he walked into a room, people noticed him, especially women.

Mike was not as tall as James, but he was a nice-looking man. His name was Michael, but friends called him Mike. When James wanted his full attention, he called him Michael. His hair was dark, but not black, longer than most men's, but not hanging long like a drug dealer. He was not as charismatic as James, but very friendly once someone approached him. He only wore a tie when required by work. His favorite outfit was blue jeans, a sport coat, and tennis shoes. At the gym he worked out daily, and it showed. He was from a wealthy family that had almost lost everything during a major downturn in the economy. His father had saved the family fortune, and someday Mike would be a rich man. But now he was just making a living for his family.

As a teenager Mike was shipped off to a military school because of his unruly behavior. There he learned a lot of gutter language and lessons in manipulating. In his early twenties, he married his first wife and divorced after their child was born. Mike always jokingly said that when his first wife asked him to marry her, her father and brothers made it clear that "no" was not an acceptable answer, considering that she was already expecting his child. Mike laughed and said the shotgun held by her father was enough motivation for immediately accepting her proposal to marry.

Mike's child-support payments kept him in and out of the courthouse constantly, even though he never missed a payment. The ex-wife was always trying to find a way to increase the child support. She was clearly an unhappy woman who constantly tried to hurt him. He thought of her as his biggest nightmare and frequently referred to her as "the Royal Bitch" rather than calling her by name. Mike managed to graduate from the state's flagship university and was accepted into law school where he completed two and a half years. The law education was cut short after a fight with another student caused him to drop out of law school. Maybe not "dropped out," but "kicked out," depending on how much he had to drink when he told the story.

THE CAPITOL HOUSE BAR

The Capitol House Bar was a gathering place for senators and representatives from the state capitol, which was located a few blocks away. Mike noticed a senator sitting in one of the booths, and that everyone who came by stopped and discussed things with him. He was like the big fish in a little pond. The senator was an important player in the bar. His name was Senator Jackson. He was a medium height, loudmouthed guy who always wore cowboy boots. His pants hung below his beer gut. He certainly was not an attractive man, but one who knew how to wheel and deal. In his hotel suite where he conducted business, he wore a house robe with black socks that almost came to his knees.

James and Mike had been to this bar before and noticed the politics of the place. The three prostitutes at the bar seemed to know everyone who walked in. One was a red-head, one a blonde, and the other one a brunette. Other than the three girls, the bar attracted mostly men.

"Look at those fucking whores," James said. "I'll bet they make more money tonight than we make in a fucking week."

"You're damn right. We don't have much of a chance against women like that."

"If we were equipped like them, just think what we could do," James said, laughing.

The blonde got off the barstool, squeezed in beside the senator in his booth, and said, "How you doing today, darling?"

The senator gave her a little kiss on the cheek and placed his hand on her leg.

"Come on, babe, we are going to rock and roll tonight," he said, amusing himself. "I just got a new prescription for that little pill that can keep you going for hours and hours, just like you like it! I know you've heard of Viagra."

Just after the senator said Viagra, the brunette jumped off her barstool and ran across the bar and grabbed the blonde by her hair, dragging her out of the booth and onto the floor. Then she kicked her in the stomach. The blonde managed to get to her feet, and they fought like two feral cats, breaking chairs and tables.

Mike jumped to his feet, followed by James, and they separated the two girls. Both continued to kick while trying to get to each other. James and Mike struggled to hold them back.

"I'll kill you, you fucking bitch," the blonde hollered. "He's supposed to be mine tonight. You had better keep your goddamn hands off of him."

Then the blonde broke loose from James and grabbed the brunette. James managed to get control of her again. The whole place was a mess.

"Girls, there's enough for all of you. There's no need to fight," the senator pleaded.

After the girls calmed down and things got back to normal, the conversation turned to who was going to pay for the girls that night.

"Smithy over there is going to pick up the tab for certain," said the old senator. Smithy was a lobbyist for a pharmaceutical firm.

The senator continued, "As a matter of fact, he's going to pay for all three girls tonight. It's going to be a ménage à trois in my suite. Drink up girls! We're leaving! Smithy owes me. I put a big one through a committee for him in the senate today. If that ole motherfucker doesn't pay you right, you tell me, and I will fix his ass at the capitol. We all know he has high pockets!"

"What are goddamn high pockets?" Mike asked James.

"High pockets means he wears his pants so high, he can't get his hands up high enough to reach into his pockets to take out cash to help with any cause," James said. "In other words, Smithy is a tightwad. He isn't going to let go of a dime he doesn't have to. Some people say that getting money from someone who's known as high pockets is like trying to squeeze blood out of a turnip."

Mike laughed. "I've never heard that before."

Smithy was a slim, average-height man who sported a goatee and looked like someone who had never been in the sun. A nerdy looking guy for certain. Surprisingly, he had a low-toned voice. He turned from the table where he was sitting near the senator's booth.

"Don't worry, Senator, I will take care of all these beautiful young ladies. They are on my tab. What you did today was a miracle."

"Damn right it was a miracle! Your company will make millions from the help I gave you today, plus the bill may even put your competitors out of business. When are you going to cut off that ugly pussy-looking mustache? Your face looks just like a pussy with that hair growing around your mouth." The senator was relentless, and knew he had the power to command anything he wanted from Smithy now.

Smithy ignored his question. "By the way, Senator, are we going to play poker in your suite tonight?"

"Smithy, you got an invitation, didn't you?"

"Yes. Eight o'clock, correct?"

"Yes, eight, you old motherfucker. You're not trying to weasel out, goddamn it, are you?"

"No sir, Senator, I will be there."

The senator's arrangement was a major source of income for the hotel, and in return it meant several thousand dollars in the senator's pocket each legislative session. It was a clever arrangement—the hotel made money by way of the senator's maneuvering state group meetings at the hotel and getting tax-exempt bonds for its renovations and remodeling. This free suite provided the senator with a little extra income each year. This income went unreported to the legislative auditors and the IRS. In return, the senator would make certain that no bill passed out of the legislature that would hurt the hotel in any way. The hotel manager was an unethical guy named Sam, who took care of covering up any activities that needed to be discreet. Sam had no problem providing the senator with falsified receipts to turn into the state for reimbursement. Sam thought of it as good government—that is, good government for Sam's hotel.

WE COULD BE LOBBYISTS

James was looking around the room analyzing each and every player. Smithy looked like a loser to him.

"We could be lobbyists," James said. "All we have to do is bullshit a few bullshitters and provide a few fucking whores and some of that marijuana your buddy out on Wilson Road is growing in his backyard. Hell, with the marijuana he's growing and a few first-class call girls like the ones sitting at the bar, we could kick ass. It won't be hard to find some whores. Women give it away easy these days. A few drinks and dinner, plus a little weed, and any man could have his way with most of them. You know the pill has changed the goddamn world."

"Look at that guy, Smithy. He has the personality of a fucking brick wall. If he can be a lobbyist, we can be great lobbyists."

"Hell, James, I heard someone say you could sell an ice-box to an Eskimo in an igloo. Certainly you or I could talk a few bullshitting legislators into voting one way or the other."

"You're right, Mike. There's no limit to what we can do with a lobbying firm. We have a little background in the law and government, and neither of us minds twisting the rules just a little bit. Both of us are good at bullshitting."

James paused before continuing. "Michael, we can't start a lobbying firm. We don't have any goddamn clients."

"Shit, we could just make up some damn clients, and they would make us look like we're important," Mike said.

"How do we make up clients?" James asked.

"We just make them up. With these phantom clients, others will come to us. You know, it's like a car salesman. When he sells a lot of cars, people think he's successful, and they go to him to buy a car."

They both laughed and Mike continued. "I think you are on to something with this lobbying firm. We could name it GOB and Associates."

"What do you mean by GOB?"

"Good Ole Boys, you know? We will be the Good Ole Boys. I understand most lobbyists make a lot of damn money."

"You're damn right! We need to get into this goddamn business. Look at that son of a bitch over there paying for the whores and drinking the best booze in the house. Look at us. We get the house brands and complain about the price."

"Do you think the other pricks in the lobbying business got in the same way, by creating imaginary clients?"

"Who knows? How in the hell else would we get into lobbying if we didn't create clients? Everyone thinks all the damn legislators are crooks, so you know the lobbyists are, too. We would fit right in with a phantom client or two."

OPTIMISTIC ORGANIZING

"OK, let's shake hands on it. We're going to do it," Mike said.

"We need to lay out a plan so we can at least look organized. We should start by creating GOB and Associates Corporation," James said.

"Shit, that costs money," Mike added. "We will have to get one of those damn overpaid lawyers involved."

"No, Mike, I think I saw a form for incorporating over at Office Depot on Northwest Boulevard. We could copy that," James said.

"OK, James, let's do it. You go over there and pick up the form. I will check with whomever at the state we need to file that damn paper with."

"It's a deal! This could be a big winner for both of us," James said.

"I'll meet you for lunch tomorrow, and we will see where we are," Mike said.

"No, I can't meet you for lunch. I have to go to court and pay that goddamn speeding ticket I got last week. Do you know anyone who can fix a ticket?" James asked.

Mike shrugged his shoulders, "No, sorry, I don't."

"I'll meet you at the bar over on Second Street that has free hors d'oeuvres if you buy a drink anytime after four p.m.," James suggested.

"How about we meet at five thirty...no, make it four thirty. We could have more free food that way," Mike said.

"Goddamn, Mike, you're always trying to save a penny. OK, four thirty at the bar called Innocence." James thought for a second. "No, on second thought, let's come back here to the Capitol House Bar. It might be interesting to see what the old senator is up to tomorrow. We need to make an effort to learn everything we can about the lobbying business. By hanging out where the lobbyists and the legislators are, we may be able to make some important connections."

"Plus, we might get to see another catfight," Mike said as he laughed.

"That works for me. See you here tomorrow," James said as they left the bar.

The next day as planned, James and Mike met at the Capitol House Bar. Mike was staring at the three whores at the other end of the bar when James walked in. Before James could sit down, Mike said, "It's a good thing we're both married, or we might be over there trying to pick up one of those girls."

"Maybe you," James said, "but not me."

James had the corporation papers, and Mike had made a few phone calls about becoming a lobbyist.

"Did you know that we have to register at the capitol, James?"

"No, I didn't know that."

"Yes, and we have to have a form signed by the clients giving us permission to represent them. That form has to be notarized. How in the hell are we going to handle that?"

"Well, our first client will be the Acupuncture Association."

"Acupuncture Association. Is there such a thing?"

"No one would be interested in acupuncture," James said, "and there probably isn't such an association. We can buy one of those seals and stamp it lightly, with a fake signature on it."

"No, it would have to be a notary seal."

"I know where we can get one. I was in a lawyer's office the other day, and his seal was lying on the receptionist's desk," James said. "We could go by his office, and you could distract her, and I could borrow the damn thing. You know him, lawyer Smith; he has a one-man, one-girl office. You could go into the bathroom and call her to tell her you are having a problem with the water. She would come to see about the problem, and I could heist the damn seal. Just turn the water off under the sink, and tell her there's no water."

The next morning they called and asked if attorney Smith was in his office. The secretary told them he was not in that morning. Soon they showed up at the office and proceeded with the plan. The law office was a dull place, two rooms furnished with cheap furniture and a bathroom. One room was for the all-in-one legal secretary, paralegal, legal assistant, and receptionist named Josephine, who sat at her desk facing the front door.

Josephine was a knockout with long legs and a perfect body—a green-eyed, bleached blond, Marilyn Monroe type with an overly friendly personality. Depending on how a person perceived her, she could be thought of as trailer trash or high class. She was definitely a woman who attracted men, maybe for a one-night stand, but she definitely got their attention. She had earned an associate degree in business administration from the local junior college during her early twenties. While working on her degree, she had an affair with one of her professors, and she's still in love with him. She thought of him often. After that affair she never had another long-term relationship with a man. Behind her were ugly, gray filing cabinets. The office certainly did not reflect a successful attorney. Mike went into the bathroom and called for help. James quickly pocketed the seal, and they told the secretary to tell the lawyer they would see him another day.

Outside the building James said, "Mike, that girl looks pretty good. She's a big-tit bitch who dresses like a girl who likes to have fun. Did you notice how low-cut her blouse was?"

"I did. How could I miss those tits? My God, they were almost hanging out. She's probably not more than twenty-seven or twenty-eight years old. She could possibly be thirty. Do you think she would be interested in helping us get started?"

"I don't know. Let's go back and invite her for drinks this afternoon."

They turned and walked back into the office, both turning on their charm and personalities.

"Josephine, would you like to have drinks with a couple of good ole boys this afternoon over at the Capitol House Bar?" Mike asked.

"Why, sure, it would be fun being with a couple of good ole boys. I need a break from this damn stressful law practice."

That afternoon at four thirty, Josephine showed up at the Capitol House Bar. She drank straight-up dirty martinis—shaken, not stirred—and the good ole boys were happy to provide them. After the second martini, she told James she would like to take him home with her for a nightcap. She didn't mind talking about how she loved sex and could go both ways. Men were her favorite, but she would make love to a beautiful woman any day. Some would consider Josephine a nymphomaniac.

James and Mike both laughed about how the martinis affected her, but they knew they might have found the woman they needed to help with their Good Ole Boys lobbying firm.

Give her a few martinis, and she became the life of the party. They might need her to entertain legislators someday. Old Senator Jackson had already invited her to sit in his booth.

He put his hand on her leg, but she removed it while politely saying, "We will have to get to know each other better, Senator, before we do that." Then she gave him a light kiss on the cheek.

Josephine was more interested in the young man who was working the crowd and wearing a bow tie and black-and-white spectator shoes as he made his way to a seat at Mike and James's table. She walked back to the table with Mike and James and introduced herself to the young man. His name was Brian. Brian went both ways and would've gone home with Mike, James, or Josephine. He was also about twenty-five. Within a few minutes, Josephine and Brian were in a taxi headed for Josephine's apartment, leaving Mike and James at the bar.

Josephine laughed as they departed. "We are going to do a little introductory fornication."

Judging from the short conversation, James and Mike realized that both Brian and Josephine were likely bisexual and loved to get naked with someone or almost anyone. They both would make out with a male or female and were not highly selective in their choice of partners.

The next day after using the seal, James and Mike went by lawyer Smith's office. While James made small talk with Josephine to distract her, Mike placed the seal back on her desk. They told her what they were doing and about the business they were trying to start.

"I might be able to help you," she said. After picking up the seal on her desk, Josephine said, "I could be your first client. I have a secretarial service I run on weekends, and you could list me as a client."

"That would be wonderful," Mike said. "You would have to sign a paper and have it notarized saying we could represent you."

"That's no problem, boys. Give me the paper, and I'll have lawyer Smith notarize it."

As he started for the door, James said, "I have one in the car. Let me go get it."

They gave Josephine the forms and said the appropriate good-byes. On their way out the door, Josephine said, "Thanks for bringing the seal back. I knew you would."

They all laughed, and the GOB departed for their car.

The next day Josephine was their first client. They discarded the Acupuncture Association fraudulent papers. They were now almost legitimate lobbyists. However, their only client was not a paying one.

JAMES'S STATE JOB

Mike and James were talking over a beer. Mike said, "James, you had a job in state government. You should know a lot about how lobbying works."

"No, I was not involved in lobbying. My job was just a sack of bullshit. Everyone in the building was a political appointee. I got the job because the boss needed to fill the job before the end of the fiscal year or lose the position. No one with political backing had applied, so he hired me. Even the secretarial staff members were political appointees."

"Really? How long did you work at this sack of bullshit job?"

"A long six months. During an office reorganization, a man was found in a basement office who had not been given a job assignment for the past five years, but he had been on the payroll. The place was like a welfare program for the politically connected."

"Did everyone have something to do, or were they all just fuckoffs like you?"

"The supervisors would travel to all parts of the state to do inspections of businesses, but a report was not required." James rolled his eyes and laughed. "The inspections generally consisted of lunch with and paid for by the business owner or a five-minute office discussion or maybe a tour of the business. The elected head of the agency didn't want any negative reports that might piss off the business owner because he wanted to get reelected or even run for governor. That was the only real goal of the entire agency."

"How long has this bullshit agency been going on?"

"For decades. Every now and then, the head of the agency would hold a news conference to announce an action to improve the state. This was usually just before his run for reelection."

"What was your job?" Mike asked.

"I helped with developing brochures, organizing news conferences, and other odds and ends—nothing of real importance. I didn't serve much of a purpose. The news conferences and the brochures were all for appearance's sake. Afterward, a few deadbeat employees were assigned to continue the show. They knew they were going to just put on a performance to get votes for the chief's reelection and to keep their jobs. To top off all this, the chief answered to a board, and the individuals on it were also elected. Their primary purpose was the same as the chief's or to run for another better-paying office. What a joke that place was."

They both laughed and shook their heads in dismay.

"Why did you leave a cushy job like that, James?"

"I couldn't stand sitting around doing nothing. Plus, the pay was not that good. Hell, most days my boss and I would take a two- or three-hour martini lunch. Then some of the bosses would hook up with their mistresses for the afternoon two or three times a week. The politicos who stabbed their friends in the back and who were the biggest deadbeats were the ones who got promoted."

"It sounds like you did the right thing getting out of there. What a waste of taxpayer dollars. Your so-called work experience in government might be awesome help to us someday."

"I don't think so," James said.

CHAPTER 2

THEY ARE HARD TO COME BY

FINDING CLIENTS TO REPRESENT

A few legislative committee hearings were taking place in the state capitol, but the session wouldn't start for another few months. James suggested to Mike that they attend a committee hearing just to see what was happening. Mike had seen the meeting notices in the newspaper and suggested they attend a meeting dealing with transportation issues.

This was James and Mike's first visit to the state capitol. It was a beautiful place, with marble and granite everywhere. The building was much more inviting than the tractor dealership where Mike worked or the ad agency where James worked in a cubicle. This was really uptown for these good ole boys. It was certainly different from the environments they had worked in before. James had some awareness of state buildings because he had worked in state government for a short period of time, but none as beautiful as the state capitol.

They listened to the debate and noticed a legislator who had distributed a copy of a bill to the committee and said he was going to introduce the bill during the next session. The bill was concerning truck weights. No one in the room was representing the truckers. The bill before the committee was for information only and would have an impact on how much weight they could carry. It was not hard to figure out that the truckers would not like the lower weight restrictions. The only people who testified were the transportation section bureaucrats, and they did not like truckers. They figured that trucks destroyed the roads and bridges, and the citizens paid to repair them.

After the committee hearing, James read the meeting notices posted in the hallway outside the committee room. He was looking for another hearing they could attend.

"The truckers may have a problem with the lower truck weights," Mike said. "They could possibly be a client. The truckers may not have a lobbyist and will need us."

"Hell, Mike, we don't know anything about truck weights."

"We can learn. There's a trucker who comes by the John Deere place sometimes in the morning. I'll talk to him tomorrow. He calls himself an independent trucker. I don't know what that's all about, but I'll find out tomorrow."

"Good, that will help."

The next day Mike looked up the independent trucker's address and phone number and called him. Peter was a short, heavyset man who shaved every day or two. Someone could describe him as a fifty-year-old hyperactive loudmouth, but he was the kind of man who could surprisingly persuade a group to follow him.

Mike greeted him with, "Hello, Peter, how are you doing today? This is Mike over at the John Deere place."

"Fine."

"Peter, I have heard you refer to yourself as an independent trucker."

"Yes, I'm an independent trucker."

"Would you tell me what an independent trucker is?"

"Sure, an independent trucker is a man like me who owns his own truck and contracts with companies to deliver their product."

Mike told him he had a friend who had a lobbying firm, and the lobbyist had told him that a legislator planed to introduce a bill to lower the weights on trucks the next session of the legislature.

"Those sons of bitches are doing it to us all the time. They fuck us every time they meet. We can hardly make a goddamn living now."

"Peter, you need to hire my friend as a lobbyist. He knows what he's doing and has represented several groups in the past. Let me set up a meeting with him for you."

"OK, that would be great."

Mike called James to report the results of his talk with Peter.

"I have a meeting set up for us this Friday at four o'clock with a man who is an independent trucker. We need to develop a color brochure real fast so we can impress him."

"Good! Let's start on it tonight."

So they quickly worked up a brochure, and James went by his ad agency later that night and printed it. James, like Mike, was always trying to save a buck. James told his boss the next day he had printed a small color print job for a friend and that the friend would be willing to pay for the printing.

"No problem," the boss said. "I'm glad to help him. Don't worry about paying. It's on the house."

FIRST REAL CLIENT

On Friday as planned, they met with Peter. There was a problem. Peter was impressed by the brochure and wanted James to represent the independent truckers, but there was no money. What a situation! They now had a real client with real issues, but the client didn't have any money to pay them. Peter offered to get a group of his independent trucker friends together to see if they would put up some money to pay James.

"I can announce a meeting on my CB radio and ask others to pass it on. If they're going to lower the weights on our trucks, there will be a bunch of us truckers out there pissed off."

The next day Mike secured a meeting place at a local second-rate hotel. He promised the hotel manager that the truckers would hold their convention there if the manager would give them a free room to meet. The manager not only complied, but he offered soft drinks and cookies for those in attendance. Mike had no idea how many would attend, but he told the hotel staff there would be about fifty people.

Mike called Peter and told him where the room was and suggested that he start announcing the meeting on his CB radio once every hour of each day. Peter did just that. Other truckers passed it on to others.

Only about forty truckers showed up for the meeting, but it was a start.

James could preach like a Baptist preacher on Sunday morning when he knew almost everyone in the congregation had sinned the night before. He truly had a gift for gab.

The next problem was that James and Mike did not know any politicians other than the state senator they had met at the Capitol House Bar. That didn't stop them. At the meeting James claimed he was a personal friend of the governor. He claimed the governor had asked him to be the chief of transportation, but he was making too much money as a lobbyist to take on a job as a bureaucrat. Mike laughed to himself because he knew James was not making a damn dime as a lobbyist.

James explained that his fees were high because so many people wanted him to lobby for them because of his connection with the governor. He said his father had been in the trucking business, and he would like to help the truckers. So in memory of his deceased father, he was going to do it for less money just for them. Lobbying a weight bill was going to take a lot of time, so he needed them to put up as much money as each of them could afford.

He looked over at Mike. "Mike, would you pass a hat around and let these boys chip in? We are going to go kick ass at the legislature."

Before the offering plate went from hand to hand around the room, and before James could call for contributions like a Baptist preacher on Sunday morning, as planned, Josephine from the law office stood up.

"Here's five thousand dollars my boss told me to contribute," she said in a loud voice.

Then Brian, dressed in a blue denim work shirt and without his spectator shoes and bow tie, stood up.

"I have three thousand my company would like to put in the pot. We can't let those bastards run over us, and I believe the GOB can stop them. My company has had enough of this legislative bullshit. It's hard enough to make a living without that bunch of assholes at the capitol constantly changing the rules. Our company is goddamn tired of them there bastards picking on us."

This started the ball rolling.

Mike passed the hat, and the men started reaching for their wallets as James encouraged them. He told those who were giving by check to make it out to GOB and Associates. They were absolutely shocked to find out they had collected more than fifteen thousand dollars, not including Josephine and Brian's fake contributions, and this was only the first meeting.

After counting the money, Peter said, "This is a good start. We'll try to get some other truckers to chip in. All truckers are tired of being run over by this bunch of goofball representatives at the capitol."

By the end of the month, after eight meetings conducted in different sections of the state, GOB had collected more than $185,000. That was more than $90,000 each and a few coins for Josephine and Brian's performances. Mike and James could tell their bosses to "take this job and shove it" and work on the lobbying firm full time.

They couldn't believe what a lucrative business they had gotten into, and all they were doing was bullshitting about legislation and passing around the hat. They were not even certain whether the legislator who talked about introducing a bill to lower truck weights would introduce it or not. If he did introduce it, and if they could win for the truckers, then they were in business. But they could also lose, and that was likely.

"You realize neither of us knows what in the shit we're doing. Are we going to report all the money to the IRS, Mike?" James asked.

"Hell, no, we are not going to report it to anyone. We passed the hat and no one knows how much money we collected," Mike said.

"I understand there's an ethics board we should report to," James said.

"Those assholes will never know what we collected, James. Just ignore them."

"OK, but we could have trouble later," James said.

Not knowing what they were doing did not stop them. They knew they needed to recruit more clients.

"It's going to be hard to find another group of stupid bastards like truckers who are willing to give two assholes like us that much money and expect no accounting of it. My God, Mike, can you believe it?"

They made up the name State Independent Truckers Association and had Peter sign it as the president of the organization. Josephine had lawyer Smith notarize the same form she had signed, and GOB submitted it to the state agency where lobbyists register. Now they were real registered lobbyists with two clients.

"Except for a few quirks, we are really in the lobbying business, James. Other than one falsified client, Josephine, we're legitimate."

They had already made more money bullshitting a few truckers than they made all year at what James called their worthless jobs.

Mike, thinking about those who had helped them, said, "James, we need to give Josephine some money to keep her interested. She can be a great asset. If we give her five thousand dollars, it would be a big bonus for her. You know she doesn't make much in that law office."

"Let's not be too generous. Make it twenty-five hundred plus all the martinis she can drink," James said.

"Hell, yeah, you're right! Twenty-five is enough. We need to keep that girl working for us," Mike said. "With those big tits, members of the house and senate are all going to be putty in her hands. She's a charmer. She could also be our part-time bookkeeper someday."

"You're right; let's do it."

"OK, we will take Brian to lunch, tell him thanks, and give him two or three hundred dollars for his effort. He's not that important to us."

That night at the Capitol House Bar, James nodded his head toward old Senator Jackson and asked Mike, "Do you think all the members are like him, out to get laid and to get whatever he can put in his pocket?"

Before Mike could answer, James continued, "Do you think some of them are honest?"

"Hell no, they're all fucking crooks."

"Every month or so, I hear on the news that one of them is on the take or is being investigated. We just need to get them where they trust us enough to do business with us. You know the FBI is pretty aggressive when it comes to legislators on the take. The feds don't seem to be concerned about whores or a few drinks. I think the FBI is only interested in large amounts of money being transferred, and we're not in that game yet."

"You're right. We will be small fish in a big pond."

TIME TO CELEBRATE

Discussing what to do next and looking for sources for new clients one afternoon at the capitol coffee shop, the conversation shifted to social affairs and a reason to celebrate.

"I've never met your wife, James. Let's take our wives out to celebrate the signing of the Independent Truckers Association at that new expensive restaurant off of Jones Avenue, Louie's. I understand they serve wonderful martinis, and the food is to die for."

"OK, how about we meet you there at seven? I'm headed home for the day."

"Good, see you there at seven."

The weather was terrible, and the streets were flooded in some parts of town, but despite the bad weather, they met at seven as planned in the foyer of Louie's new upscale restaurant. Both had nice-looking wives, but Mike's wife, Catherine, was a beauty. She was a dignified lady, immaculate dresser, stylish, and well spoken. James hadn't told Mike that he and his wife were separated—not legally, but they didn't live under the same roof. They had only been separated for about four months, and James was living with a friend. Although separated, they still went out together and pretended to be married. They remained good friends.

"Catherine, you haven't met my wife, Sarah, have you?" James asked.

"No, she's beautiful. It is so nice to meet you, Sarah."

Sarah smiled. "It's nice to meet you too."

The hostess said, "There'll be a forty-five-minute wait. You may wait in the bar, if you like." Once in the bar, they each ordered a martini: up, dry, and certainly not the rotgut house brand. Mike started the conversation.

"Where did you two meet?" Mike always started conversations with new friends this way. He thought it was something people always liked to talk about.

"James and I met in church, the Baptist church over on Saint Michael Street."

James sat quietly, knowing that she was lying. They had actually met at an office pool party where everyone swam naked. It was an office sex orgy.

When James asked the same question, Mike was more open and honest. He said, "Do you remember that place where you could rent a hot tub by the hour off Turner Avenue? Well, I was working for a lumber dealer and called on the business. The office was having a hot tub party after work that day. Catherine, the office manager, invited me to join them. I'll never forget it, because they smoked marijuana and drank that cheap wine. She was the prettiest woman in the tub. We married two weeks later."

"How long have you been married?" James asked.

"Five happy years," Catherine said.

"We have been married four years," Sarah said. "We went to New York City on our honeymoon."

Mike said, "Catherine and I were so poor, and neither of us would allow our parents to help with the honeymoon when we married, so we didn't go on a honeymoon. Later we went to the British Virgin Islands for a week. That was fun.

We chartered a sailboat and enjoyed sailing it. I was married once before and have one child, and she was also married once before and has two children."

Mike laughed and made his usual statement about his first wife. "When my first wife, Marguerite, asked me to marry her, her father encouraged me to agree. I'm surprised we were married as long as we were. The marriage only lasted until the baby came."

Sarah said, "I was married before but had no children. I am James's first wife."

James added, "And my last."

Catherine rolled her eyes, but made a cheerful, bright face. "It's amazing how much we have in common." They all raised their glasses and made a toast to happy marriages.

After dinner Mike expressed his opinion of the night, saying, "This has been fun. Maybe we should do it every week."

"Yes, Friday nights," Catherine said. "There's rarely anything to do on Friday nights except watch television."

Mike proclaimed immediately, "You know we can write these dinners off our income taxes."

James added, "Yes, but we will need to put down a legislative staffer's name or a legislator and claim that we were entertaining him."

LOCATION, LOCATION, LOCATION— THE GREENHOUSE

"What we need to do next is find more clients," James said to Mike. They had become fixtures in the state capitol coffee shop and cafeteria. The coffee shop was a simple 1950s

The Lobbyist

environment. The glass walls facing the elevators in the capitol made it possible for those having coffee to see who was moving around the capitol building. The place needed painting and was not the cleanest establishment in the world. It felt like an area that had been neglected.

A short, fat, grumpy, elderly man who rarely had a nice word to say to anyone managed it. Strangely, he seemed to like James and Mike and would sometimes sit at their table and talk to them. They bought coffee for the bureaucrats or anyone who would tell them about the functions of the legislature. The Good Ole Boys were just nice guys looking for information.

They were beginning to make a lot of friends around the capitol, especially among the bureaucrats. Because the session would start soon, the state employees on the legislative staff were busy drafting bills that would be introduced during the first five days of the session. Some bills had been prefiled. James and Mike were hoping for an inside track on which groups or companies were going to need a lobbyist for the session.

THE GREENHOUSE PURCHASE

Mike called James, and they agreed to meet for lunch the next day. Mike told James they needed to get a small office to work out of. His wife did not like him hanging around the house all day. It was as if she were having an affair or something like that and didn't want him around.

"We must keep our expenses down," James said. "Maybe we can find a cheap one- or a two-room office near the capitol."

"OK, let's start looking this afternoon."

An older neighborhood surrounded the capitol. Most of the buildings were run down. There were no "Office for Rent" signs anywhere, except one located about a block and a half from the capitol. The "For Rent" sign was on a poorly maintained vacant house that was painted pale green.

As they stood in front of the old house, Mike said to James, "We may have to rent this old house. It can't rent for much, especially since it's painted shitty green."

"It appears we are going to be doing most of our business in the state capitol coffee shop," James said. "A fancy office is not important to us, other than as a place to hang our hats and make a few phone calls. One lobbyist told me he operated out of his garage."

They knocked on the door of one of the neighbors and asked if anyone knew anything about the house. The lady who came to the door was about forty years old, thin, hair down to her shoulders, and dressed like a flower child. A real flower child, like one you would have seen at Woodstock. The only thing missing was a joint in her hand. She stood behind the screen door and answered their questions. Her place looked dark inside. She told them the house next door had been vacant for the past three years, and some dopers had been going in there smoking pot. Kids had used it occasionally for a hangout.

Then she said, "Why would anybody want that place? It would take a month to clean it up." They had called the number on the "For Rent" sign, but did not get an answer.

They asked her if she knew the phone number of the owner.

"Yes, I have his phone number. Give me a minute, and I'll get it for you guys." She went inside and came back with the number she had written on a small piece of paper. "What are you boys wanting to do with this house?"

"We are lobbyists, and we would like to make a small office out of it," James said.

"That's nice," she said. "You can use my phone to call the landlord. His name is Roger."

Mike called the number, and Roger's wife answered. Mike started the conversation. "We would like to look at the house you have downtown."

"My husband died a month ago, and I don't have a key to get into it."

"We noticed the back door is open. Would it be OK if we walk through it?"

"Yes, sir. Go right ahead."

"How much do you want for the house?" James asked.

"I'll take anything to get rid of it," she said loudly.

"OK, we'll take a look at it."

James thanked the lady at the door, and they went next door and into the house. It was a rat's nest. It had one big open room with an outdated but usable kitchen in one corner, two bedrooms, and a bathroom behind that.

"She could never sell this place without putting a lot of money into it," Mike said. "Maybe we should lowball her an offer and clean and paint it ourselves. Hell, James, we have enough cash. We could offer her maybe, twenty thousand dollars? They say this part of town is coming back. If it doesn't work out, we could flip it."

James paused for a minute and said, "OK, Mike, but we have to get some more clients, or we are going to have to keep our worthless fucking jobs. Try offering her fifteen thousand first."

They called the lady back and asked her if they could come talk to her. Upon arrival at her house, Mike concocted a story about how they wanted the house for his aging mother. They couldn't afford much, but they would pay her $15,000 for the place if she would agree to finance it for them. They told her they would pay her $150 a month.

They were both surprised when she said, "Yes, I will do that for you boys. It's so wonderful that you're trying to help your elderly mother, and I don't have a use for the house."

"We don't have any money to put down, but you can depend on us paying you," Mike said.

"OK, you look like good folks," she said.

James suggested, "We should set it up to where we have a written agreement. Mike, you call Josephine and ask her to get that lawyer she works for to draw up a mortgage."

He did, and she did. Roger's widow came to the law office the next week, and the deal was done. Now Mike and James owned an office space worth more than $50,000 a few blocks from the state capitol.

"Do you feel bad robbing that old lady, James?"

"Hell no; she got a few dollars that she didn't have before. Plus, if we hadn't done it, one of those real estate agents would have. We just got to her first. Hell, she's happy."

For the next two weeks Mike, James, Catherine, and Sarah spent several hours a day cleaning, scrubbing, and painting the office. James was amazed how Sarah helped when she knew they were not likely to ever live together again. The girls decorated the office with a few old lawbooks and framed newspapers showing historical legislative events. They had found the old newspapers and lawbooks in an estate sale.

GOB was on the move with only one client but looking for others. The proximity to the state capitol was beginning to look like a very positive selection. When they didn't want to brown bag or cook at their new office, they ate in the cafeteria and rubbed shoulders with the bureaucrats, as well as the representatives and senators. It would be easy to attend every committee hearing and look for another group that was unrepresented.

"We need to get an accountant to tell us how to do accounting things," James suggested to Mike. "I am still worried about the IRS and the ethics board."

"I know one who is a state auditor, and a friend told me he is the best. When he does your income tax, he asks how much you want to pay, you tell him, and he makes sure your 1040 form fits your desired payments. One man said when he asked Jimmy, the CPA, how much one plus one was, he answered, 'How much do you want it to be?' Believe it or not, he's a real certified CPA."

"That sure sounds like our man. Could you set up a meeting with him next week?" James asked.

"Yes. I don't have his phone number, but I will call my friend and get it. It'll have to be after four thirty early next week because he works for the state during the day."

"That's OK, after four thirty is fine."

WHAT A WELCOMING

At the office, James said, "Look, we got mail." He held up several envelopes for Mike to see. "These are our first pieces of mail received by GOB and Associates. They look official. I wonder what's in them."

"Open them and see," Mike said.

"Oh, they are invitations from senators and representatives," James said.

"How nice. I guess someone must have told them we are in the lobbying business and they're welcoming us," Mike said.

"Hell, Mike, these are not welcoming us. These are solicitations for money—a lot of money. This guy wants us to attend a fund raiser hosted by his reelection committee. The asshole is asking us to send a check for $5,000 made out to his reelection committee, and we don't even know the son of a bitch. I wonder where he got our name and address?"

Mike took the invitation from James's hand, looked at it, and said sarcastically, "At least a steak dinner is offered, along with an open bar."

"Goddam, a $5,000 steak! That's expensive!" James yelled.

"Here's another one," Mike said as he held it up for James to see. "She's a senator and the chairperson of the health and welfare committee. The invitation has a long list of supporters on it. She wants $3,000 and is offering nothing but adding the GOB to her list of supporters. There's not even a party to attend."

"This one is not so bad," James said. "He wants $500 and he's serving beer and barbecue in a park."

"Holy shit, this one wants $20,000 per person to reelect the governor. They are only serving cocktails, but it's hosted by Willie Nelson."

"Hell, we can't afford this. I thought all we had to do was bullshit bullshitters, but this bullshitting costs money, lots of money. Judging from these invitations, we're going to have to pay just to talk to them. Can you believe this shit?" James exclaimed.

"No, one of these invitations costs more than the Greenhouse, and there will likely be more of them next week," Mike said. "If we contribute to all these sons of bitches we will be out of money in a month."

"We will just ignore all of them, but hold onto the invitations. We may have to attend some of them," James said.

The next week more invitations came. "They must've gotten our address off the lobbyist registration form we submitted to the state ethics board," Mike said.

"You're right. That's the only place we have used the Greenhouse address," James said. "This means all lobbyists are receiving the invitations."

"Hell, they won't notice if we don't respond," Mike said.

The next day the telephone started ringing. James answered the phone and told the callers that the GOB was new to the lobbying business and did not have the money at this time, but to please keep them on the list. He told each caller that they would like to help the candidate in the future.

They were surprised that four of the callers told them to come as guests of the candidate, and they did just that.

MINGLING WITH TED BUNDY

James had met a female bureaucrat in the coffee shop early one morning while she was having breakfast. From the conversations he thought she was going to be very helpful. James was attracted to her right away. She was tall but not as tall as James. She was a beautiful woman with a lot of elegance and class about her. For some reason James thought she didn't look like she belonged in the state capitol as a state employee. He was interested in knowing more about her and asked for her phone number, but she wouldn't give it to him.

"I will have to know a lot more about you before I give you my phone number," she said. Then she laughed and said, "What is your social security number and bank account number? At what bank do you do business?"

"That's a little more information than girls usually request. You sound like a real gold digger."

She laughed and said, "A gold digger! A girl has to be careful nowadays. Have you heard of Ted Bundy?"

"Are you comparing me to Ted Bundy?"

"Well, he was good-looking just like you."

"Thanks, at least you think I'm good-looking. Maybe a mass murderer, but good-looking."

"Well, it's true, you are a very good-looking, attractive man."

They both laughed. She gave him her office number and told him to call her anytime, and she would try to help him. Her name was Kimberly, and she worked as a bill drafter on the legislative staff. James had no idea how the woman he had just met would change his life forever.

The next time James saw her in the coffee shop, he invited her for a drink at the Capitol House Bar. She thought about the invitation for a minute, making James wonder if she would accept.

Then she said, "Are you inviting me because you think I'm a beautiful and attractive woman, or are you just lobbying me for information?"

"Both."

"Well, you're an honest man. OK, that sounds like it could be fun."

"I'll meet you at the front door of the state capitol at four forty-five, Miss Kimberly."

"See you there, James."

James was at the front door of the capitol at four fifteen. He did not want to miss her. After greeting her on the capitol steps, they walked to the Capitol House Bar, where Mike and James had become regulars. The GOB did not have to order drinks at the Capitol House Bar because when they walked up to the bar, the bartender knew them and would say, "Your regular?"

They would respond, "Yes."

Kimberly noticed this and said, "Oh, you hang out here a lot, or you drink a lot when you are here. Even old Senator Jackson seems to know you."

James replied defensively, "We come in here so we can talk to legislators and lobbyists and learn more about the business. Senator Jackson told Mike about two groups that needed a lobbyist. The lobbyist Smithy, who works for a pharmaceutical company, told us he might hire us to assist him on a few bills. There seem to be more legislative decisions being made here than at the capitol."

Although Kimberly had been on the legislative staff for only a short period of time, she had learned a lot. She and James hit it off. She was a natural blonde with blue eyes that could penetrate a man's soul, and she knew how to use them.

Kimberly said, "We are attracting a lot of attention in here. James, I want to give you a piece of advice. Don't ever let these people know how you think or with whom you associate."

James thought about what she said. "I'm sorry, would you like to get out of here? We could go to my office; it's only a couple of blocks away. I have vodka there, and I make a mean martini."

"Yes, let's get out of here."

As they walked, he asked, "Rather than my office, how about dinner? Jack's Bistro, the new restaurant, is just up the street.

"Yes, that would be nice."

"We will take a table out of the spotlight."

James was sensitive to her concern about overexposure to people involved in the legislative process. The couple continued walking up Third Street to Jack's, where they were the only customers in the entire place. Still, they took a seat at a table for two in the back. They talked for hours. Kimberly told James about the legislature. It was like a cram course for James. She was providing more information than he ever imagined getting from one person—things such as why certain words were used in bills, who the best bill drafter was, scheduling, who had an agenda, those to avoid, and adjournment of the legislature. She showed him in simple terms how a bill managed to make its way through the legislature.

She explained to James that lobbyists seem to break down into three groups. First, she told James, the independent lobbyists are generally the grassroots lobbyists. These lobbyists would work for anyone and for any purpose, whether they believed in the goal of the client or not. They used the local political connections of individuals in the group to influence legislation. They worked for multiple individuals, associations, or corporations. She pointed out that the GOB firm complied with this definition.

Moving right on, Kimberly talked about association lobbyists, who were the full-time employees of an association for the purpose of influencing legislation. They also assumed a title, such as executive director of the organization. They managed the affairs of the group. Depending on the size of the association, the lobbyists might be full time or part time.

James asked the waiter for a pen and paper and took notes as Kimberly talked. She pointed out that the lobbyist named Smithy was a corporate lobbyist. Corporate lobbyists were employees of a company, such as a pharmaceutical, electrical, or insurance company; they kept track of legislation and tried to influence the outcome. Sometimes they were employed by cities to make certain state legislation did not negatively affect the city. Then she confused James by saying that some lobbyists fit into all three categories. There were others, but most fit into these categories.

James would have paid thousands for this crash course. After another martini the conversation got more personal. She told him she was not dating anyone and had never been married, but she had had several failed relationships. She told him she had no interest in a relationship with a man, and if he was after sex, he was barking up the wrong tree. He assured her he wasn't. He told her he was married and about his wife and what a wonderful person she was. He failed to tell her that he was separated from his wife. They agreed their relationship would not include sex. They would just be friends.

After dinner they staggered out of the restaurant and down the dark street. As they walked, he put his hand across her shoulder as if trying to make certain she did not fall. Kimberly put her arm around his waist, and they laughed and talked as they walked. It was raining slightly, and an observer could easily imagine they were children playing in a summer rain. James bought a newspaper and held it over Kimberly's head. Someone seeing them would think they were lovers, or at least old, best friends. He walked Kimberly to her car, which was located in the lot next to the state capitol in a reserved parking space.

"I thought these reserved places were just for senators and representatives."

"Yes, they are, unless you know the right person, James."

"We have had too much to drink to drive. Let's sit on the capitol steps and let the alcohol work its way out of our system."

"OK," she agreed.

They took a seat about halfway up the steps. A weather front had come through, and the rain had stopped. The clouds cleared, and it was a beautiful spring night. The stars were bright as they listened to the city noises at a distance. James told her about his family, three brothers and one sister, all earning college degrees from the state university. She listened as he talked about his childhood and about the hardships his family went through during one of the economic downturns. He also told her about the good times. Kimberly was a good listener. When he quit talking, she asked questions to keep him talking. After a while, they decided enough time had passed to process the excess alcohol, and it was OK to drive.

"I truly enjoyed the night with you, Kimberly. You're a wonderful person. Let's plan to do this again next Monday."

"OK, I'd like that."

"Same time, same place. OK with you?"

"Yes," she replied.

"Thanks for all the help. You're the greatest, Miss Kimberly."

She laughed at his use of the term "Miss Kimberly" and said, "This has been one of the nicest evenings I've had in a long time."

"You be careful on the way home, Kimberly."

He walked back to his office and sat in his chair for a few minutes, thinking about the night. What a nice and beautiful person he had met. He regretted not telling her he and his wife had agreed to separate and that he was not living with her.

When James arrived home, his roommate said, "Where have you been? It's twelve thirty at night."

"Oh, I took a gorgeous lady who works on the legislative staff to dinner, and then we had a few drinks," James said.

His roommate, a high school friend he was sharing an apartment with, said, "You look like you had more than just a few."

"Hell, it was a productive night. She told me about a list of organizations that might need a lobbyist, plus she told me where to get the names of people who started the groups that sometimes use lobbyists. I didn't know it, but there is a state office that has a list of nonprofit organizations with the names of the people who incorporated each organization. Mike doesn't know it yet, but he and I are going to that office tomorrow to get the list and contact each and every one of them. We have to get new clients, or we will go broke fast. You will be putting me on the street for failure to pay my share of the rent."

The roommate said, "You're right."

A LITTLE GERMAN BAR

First thing the next morning, James called Kimberly. She answered on her direct line. "Hello."

"I certainly enjoyed last night," he said.

"I enjoyed it too."

"This morning I'm going to meet Mike, and we're going to the state office you told me about to follow up on that list of names and groups. Thanks for telling me where we could find the list of organizations that might need a lobbyist. You have been so helpful. I feel like I've known you for a long time, even though you didn't tell me much about yourself."

"I feel the same way, James. Isn't that interesting? I bet you left out a few things that you wanted to tell me but didn't know how to say them."

"I'm not sure what you're talking about, but you are probably correct."

They continued with small talk until James heard Mike come up the front steps of the little house/office. "I have to go. My partner just came in. I look forward to seeing you again. Next Monday, same time, same place?"

"No, not the Capitol House Bar, James. How about the little German bar located down at the end of Main Street? It's not far from your office, and I won't have to look at all those senators and representatives I have to work with every day," Kimberly said.

"OK, and I'll let you know what Mike and I find out after we get the list from the state office you told me about."

"OK, James. I will see you Monday at four forty-five at the front door of the state capitol."

BUYING THE LIST

That morning James told Mike what he had done the night before and how helpful the lady was during dinner. James never mentioned the lady's name, and Mike never asked. They went to the state office at ten o'clock and asked for a copy of the list.

The person working behind the counter said, "This list is extensive. It will cost you twenty cents per page."

"OK," Mike said.

They received the list of several hundred nonprofit associations that might need a lobbyist.

"We need several friends like the lady who told you about the list. My God, what a list! It's going to take two months to call all these people," Mike happily complained.

They divided the list and started calling all the associations. Most told them they did not use a lobbyist but would listen to what they had to say. Occasionally they would come across one that said, "Yes, we need a lobbyist, but we don't have the money to pay for one."

Others said, "We have a group of volunteers who go to the legislature and represent our organization." After three days of calling, they had only one scheduled meeting.

Brian gave Mike the phone number of a theater manager to call.

"The theaters may be interested in hiring a lobbyist to pass a bill," Brian said. He laughed and told Mike he had met Bruce, the theater manager, at an orgy.

Mike thought he was joking, but he told James that Brian might be serious. Mike set up a meeting with the theater manager to discuss what they needed.

THE CELLAR BAR

James met Kimberly at the front door of the capitol, and they went to the little German bar on Third Street named the Cellar Bar. The place was small and dark, with cobwebs and beer mugs on the wall. Every piece of art in the place represented something from the Old World. One or two pieces looked like fine pieces of art, the others worthless. The owner, who was also the bartender, janitor, and cook, had a patch over his left eye and talked with a heavy German accent. He had a small tattoo on the back of his left hand. The whole place made James feel like he was in old Europe, although he'd never been there.

"How did you find this place?" James asked Kimberly.

"It's been around for years. He doesn't have much business, and most people don't know about it."

They sat at the bar, which only had four barstools, rather than at one of the three small tables.

"What would you like to drink?" the old German asked.

James looked at Kimberly and asked, "A martini?"

"Of course! Up and dirty, please!"

James replied, "The same for me."

"Smirnoff?" asked the German.

"No, Absolute."

"I don't have that brand. How about a Russian vodka?"

"OK, that will be interesting," James said.

The old German bar owner grumbled under his breath just so they could barely hear, "Smirnoff is better." The German was so close behind the bar that they could reach out and touch him. There was only a small walking path between the bar and the counter behind it.

James quizzed the German. "How long have you been in the United States?" The German paused for some time and avoided the answer. The three of them talked about old Germany, the war, and the bar itself. After a few minutes, Kimberly and James moved to one of the tables in the corner of the small room. The old German went into the back where his little office was located, as if he was trying to give the couple some privacy.

Later that evening, James and Kimberly walked back to her car and sat on the capitol steps and talked about government, lobbying, and life in general. The weather was chilly, so James took his coat off, and Kimberly leaned against him so his jacket would cover both of them. James questioned Kimberly about her background, but she only provided what she wanted him to know. She had learned that providing too much information was not a good idea. Other men had tried to take advantage of her when she provided more information than necessary. She had learned this lesson the hard way. She knew deep in her soul that James was not that kind of man, but she had to be certain before she completely opened up.

EARLY BIRDS AT THE GREENHOUSE

Realizing that their futures could depend on being successful in the lobbying business, Mike and James decided after buying the Greenhouse to start each morning with breakfast to discuss what they had learned the day before and how they were progressing. It would be an informal breakfast meeting of sorts. They were both early birds, and breakfast at the office around seven o'clock every workday played well for each of them. By meeting early they would avoid the morning traffic rush and be able to talk before the staff arrived, if they ever had a staff. Afterward they could go to the capitol coffee shop, or work in the office or wherever they needed to be that day. This was a way of keeping their focus on business. The old kitchen needed replacing, but it would do for now.

THE OFFICE, BY WAY OF THE CELLAR

The next Monday James and Kimberly had been to the Cellar Bar again and were walking back to the capitol. He said, "We're going to be walking near my office. Would you like to see it?"

"Yes, I would," she said.

"It's not much, but it's a start," he said. "We bought the building from an old lady. We got a real deal on it. It's not completely furnished yet, but it has chairs and desks. We need a couch and a conference table. Mike's office is in one bedroom, and mine is in the other. The house has a neat little front porch. It would be nice to have some chairs on the porch, but we would have to chain them for certain. It's not the best neighborhood in the world, but it's close to the capitol. Where we're standing right now, we're only about a block from the capitol and one block from my office."

When they arrived, James opened the door with his key and held it open for Kimberly to enter.

She looked around the room and said, "This is wonderful, and it can be beautiful."

She laughed when she noticed a Mickey Mouse telephone on one of the tables.

"The old fireplace is very nice. Does it work?" she asked.

"We don't know. We'll try it this winter."

"You'd better have it checked out, or you might burn the house down," she warned.

"Yes, you're right. We will."

Kimberly proceeded to the first office down the left side of the hallway, which was Mike's office.

Then she went on down the hallway, and he said, "This one is mine." He walked through the door and said with a big smile, "Welcome; come on in."

Inside she examined every little item in his office, commenting on each one.

"Do you think a man and a woman can really be just friends?" he asked.

"Yes," she replied. Then she added, "I have men friends. No sex involved. James, you're thinking about sex, aren't you?"

"Absolutely not. What made you think that?" He boasted in a loud tone.

"Your question," she answered.

"Well, you are a nice-looking woman."

"You're not so bad yourself, but we need to move on to another subject. Oh, here's one of your brochures. It's colorful. May I have one?"

"Yes, you may have one. There are only a few lies in it."

"It's very nicely done." She took a seat in James's chair behind his desk. "I think I could be a lobbyist."

James took a seat in front of his desk and said, "Yes, you could."

"I don't think so, but it's fun to watch you guys operate."

"What makes a good lobbyist?" James asked.

She hesitated for a minute. "A good lobbyist has to discard any thoughts he might have of being politically idealistic. It seems there are few extremists among the lobbyists. I think a good lobbyist can be a conservative or a liberal or anywhere in between, but not extreme. He can debate or argue both sides and convince you that he believes in whatever side is needed at the time." She took a breath, thought for a minute, and then continued.

"Lobbying is similar to being a criminal defense lawyer. A good attorney can defend a criminal whom he knows is guilty. Lobbyists learn very fast that it's much easier to find a client who is polluting the air and water than it is to find one who is an environmentalist and can pay. The environmentalist may have a good cause, but he's unlikely to be able to put the money on the table for GOB and Associates. The environmental groups try to negotiate the fee down to where it is not worth your time. They don't seem to realize that lobbying is a business, and business without profit goes out of business."

"I am impressed," James said. "I never expected such a critique."

Debating was not hard for either of the Good Ole Boys to do because neither was committed to one side or the other. It was easy for both to adjust to making money from either side of politics. To them it was just a business, and they had to think in business terms.

They continued to talk about the office and politics for a few minutes, and then they proceeded on to the capitol steps, where they had sat before.

James asked her about her previous relationships, but she wasn't talking other than commenting on one man.

"There was one man I would've married, but he didn't want to marry me. I certainly loved him, but it didn't work out. He didn't want the responsibility of a woman like me."

"Responsibility? What do you mean, responsibility?"

"Oh, I must've used the wrong word. It just didn't work out. Let's go to another subject, please. He is history."

James and Kimberly's relationship was becoming more and more personal each time they went to dinner or for cocktails. He was really attracted to her, and she was attracted to him. Neither wanted to step over the line that led to sex. At least that's what they were saying to each other, but deep in the privacy of their minds, both were thinking about it. James's beeper rang.

"It is my wife beeping me. I need to call her back."

"Where are you going to tell her you are?"

I will tell her I am at the office.

"Oh, you are going to lie to your wife."

"It's best that I not tell her everything. You have a meeting in the morning, and I need to talk to her."

"You're right, James, I do have a big meeting in the morning, and I need to be prepared."

They walked to Kimberly's car. James looked her in the eye and said, "I hope we can do this again soon. Certainly, I enjoy being with you. I haven't been completely honest with you. I'm separated from my wife. I was embarrassed to tell you because I was taught by my parents that marriage was forever, but it hasn't worked out that way."

"I know you are separated from your wife. I also know that you are living with a male roommate in an apartment located at 2125 Saint Joe Street, your social security number is 555-555-5555, you bank at the First National Bank on Crowder Street, and your credit is absolutely perfect."

Surprised by her remarks, he asked, "How do you know all that?"

"I work in the state capitol. We know everything about everybody." She laughed and said, "Someday I'll let you in the loop. That is, if you're a good boy and behave yourself."

"I promise to be a good boy."

They both laughed. James gave Kimberly a hug. She responded by simultaneously hugging him lightly. James felt her breasts against his chest and wanted to squeeze her harder, but he was not certain how she would respond.

Then he said, "Good night and drive carefully. You know, we forgot to eat! Maybe next week the German will have some sauerkraut and German sausage."

Kimberly got in her car and drove away. James watched the car as the taillights faded in the distance, all the while thinking how much he liked her and wondering how she got the information about him.

PAUL THE LOBBYIST

At breakfast in the office Mike told James, "I met a black lobbyist named Paul yesterday. He is a very nice guy with years of experience, and he's really a character. You will like him. He has a laugh that is contagious. Paul represents finance companies. He also lobbies for payday check-cashing businesses—you know, the ones that charge high fees for cashing paychecks. You're going to laugh at this story that he told the group at the coffee table. It's about money and racism. There is a real message in the story. It certainly proves that it's all about money. Paul has a twisted saying: 'It's not about the money; it's about the money.'"

Mike continued, "Paul told the group he was working for one of the former governors, and the governor asked him to deliver forty thousand dollars to a hate group that was planning to have a big meeting just before Election Day. It was one of those neo-Nazi, Klansmen, or white nationalist groups or something like that. It was a close election, and the candidate for governor was trying to get every vote he could. The extremists had the power to influence a small percentage of the vote. A big gathering protesting his candidacy for governor could cost him the election because it was so close.

"Paul drove about seventy-five miles south to take the cash. He said he drove up to the meeting place, which was a barroom located several miles down a gravel road. He parked his car in front of the bar, got out, walked up three steps, and opened the door to the one-room country-western bar. Behind a long bar was a bartender pouring drinks. Six extremists were seated on the left, in the back side of the room at a table.

"The bartender picked up a shotgun from under the counter, and all six men stood up. The shotgun was pointed at Paul, and one of the extremists screamed at the top of his voice, 'What in the fuck are you doing in here, n****r?'

"Paul yelled back, 'Don't shoot,' and he held up a paper bag full of money and said he was representing the candidate. One of the men said, 'Is the fucking candidate a goddamn fool, sending a man like you to meet with us? Doesn't he know we will kill your ass?' Paul paused for a minute or so. Finally, Bobby, a lobbyist for the bankers, impatiently asked, 'What happened next?'

"'The bartender shot me in the leg,' Paul said with a serious face. Before anyone could say anything, Paul laughed and said, 'No, he didn't shoot me. I just thought he was going to shoot me.'"

Mike continued the story after taking a sip of coffee. "Paul said he just knew he was going to die. He walked aggressively straight to the table where all the extremists were standing and immediately dumped the entire paper bag of cash on the table in front of the men. The cash scattered all over the table. They looked at the money and then at Paul. After a few words were said, they invited Paul to sit at the table with them. The bartender put the shotgun back under the bar. Paul took a seat at the table and had numerous drinks. Three hours later he left the bar so intoxicated that he shouldn't have been driving.

"He said when he left the bar, he had six new best friends, all of whom belonged to some white nationalist group. They shook his hand, gave him a shoulder hug, and wished him a safe trip back to the capital city, Paul said. And the extremists didn't rally against the candidate.

"When Paul finished the story, everyone at the table fell out laughing," Mike said. "Paul concluded that it was all about money. I'm beginning to believe this whole goddamn business of politics is about nothing but greed," Mike concluded, and James agreed.

SECTION II

LIFE IS GOOD, AND THE SESSION BEGINS

CHAPTER 3

BECOMING A PLAYER IN STATE POLITICS

THINGS START HAPPENING

Mike had talked to a building materials dealer who told him to come by his office the next Wednesday at 11:00 a.m. to discuss lobbying. The dealer was located 150 miles from the capital city. Mike agreed to do just that.

James had scheduled a meeting for the next Thursday with the theater manager Brian had told them about to discuss lobbying for him.

As planned, Mike and James drove to meet with the president of the Building Materials Association. Upon arrival they learned the association had fired its lobbyist just weeks before. The lobbyist had been convicted of sexual harassment, and building materials dealers didn't want to be associated with allegations such as that. To their advantage, Mike spoke the language of materials dealers because he had worked in the business for a few years. They took a few minutes to look at this lumber dealer's place of business. Mike commented on each section, ranging from lumber to nuts and bolts.

The dealer invited them to have lunch with him at a restaurant near his office. Mike and the president of the association hit it off right away because Mike knew the terminology. The dealer also knew the man Mike had worked for and had called him for a reference before they arrived. Mike's former boss at the lumber dealership where he worked several years ago spoke highly of him.

At lunch the Good Ole Boys and Associates picked up the tab. The president of the Building Materials Association said he would like to hire them, but he wanted to know how much they expected to get paid. They told him they would accept whatever the last lobbyist was paid, thinking he would be straightforward and honest with them. They did not tell him, but the reason they would accept the fee charged by the former lobbyist was because they didn't know how much to charge. He said he would need to get approval from the board, but the group usually followed his recommendations. Two weeks later he called, and the GOB was hired.

The president of the Building Materials Association said, "The association will pay your firm eighty-five thousand dollars a year and some expenses not to exceed twenty thousand dollars. You will need to come by my office and pick up the check next week. We pay half now and the other half in six months. We also have a contract for you to sign. It's a simple contract stating that you will be responsible for your own payroll taxes and so forth. You will be considered an independent contractor."

"Yes, that's perfectly acceptable with us," Mike said. "Thank you for working with us. We will be in your office next week to sign the contract and pick up the first check. We will not disappoint you. Thanks again."

As planned, the next week they signed the contract and picked up the check. GOB now had two real paying clients and Josephine's Secretarial Service. The Building Materials Association and Independent Truckers Association were legitimate.

THE HELP VERSUS THE ELECTED

At breakfast James and Mike talked about what was said at the coffee shop gathering the day before. Bobby, a lobbyist for the bankers association was a short guy and thinner than most. He wore horn-rimmed glasses and looked like a book-worm. Someone described Bobby as the kid who carried a briefcase in junior high school. He truly enjoyed lobbying. It was like a game of strategy to him. He had talked about who is important and who isn't. Bobby spoke about statewide elected officials, the secretary of state, the state treasurer, and others as if they were unimportant. He said that knowing statewide elected officials was important only to impress clients. Rarely did they ever help you. The bureaucrats were much more important to lobbyists. One of the interesting things he said was how amazed he was to see what a lobbyist could get done through the "help." By the "help," he meant the state workers.

"You know, he is right," James said. "They are the people who carry on the day-to-day functions of government, and they have a great deal of influence on what goes to and what comes out of the legislature. They control the outcome of regulations. They write the bills and understand what one word can do to the meaning of a law. They know when to use the word *should* versus the word *shall*."

Bobby pointed out that the legislative staff is supposed to be unbiased and independent and only carry out the functions directed by the legislature. But he claimed that wasn't the way the real world was at all. Most of them had opinions and managed to cleverly insert them into bills. He said not to forget that the legislator was term limited, and the bureaucrat's job could last a lifetime. He said that overall and for the long term, the bureaucrat had the most influence in government. Mike nodded his head in agreement.

WHAT IS THE NORM?

"James, you know that guy called Donald? He's a very interesting and talented individual. I got a chance to look at some of his writing. It's excellent. Everyone says he's one of the men to go to for drugs or women. He's the legislative supplier of whores."

"Do you think that's the norm, Mike?"

"What do you mean, the norm?"

"I mean the way of doing business here. We haven't had to do anything like that, as we thought we would in the beginning. Do you think we are a minority?" James asked.

"I'm not certain." Mike thought about it for a minute and said, "No, I don't think he is the norm. I think most lobbyists are men and women of integrity who are just fascinated by the process. There are exceptions, but most of those I met are reliable and honest. Companies can't afford to be associated with people like him. Some are truly outstanding citizens and try to do what is right every time."

"Contrary to the general public's opinion of lobbyists, I think there's more honesty among legislators and lobbyists than among the members of the general public," James said.

For some reason Donald was a great help to the GOB. He explained the process, warned them about pitfalls, and generally was very helpful. A legislator at the capitol told the GOB one day that Donald's power was in the group he represented and his exceptional understanding of parliamentary procedure. He knew more about parliamentary procedure than the legislators. Legislative leaders would sometimes consult with him about the details of the process. He knew every maneuver there was to kill a bill by parliamentary procedure.

"We need to learn more about parliamentary procedure," Mike said. "It's a very good thing to know in our business."

"Donald is a very talented writer and has a degree in journalism," James said.

"Journalism is an excellent background for a lobbyist."

"You're right," Mike added.

"Are you saying that because you have a degree in journalism?"

James laughed and said, "What would make you think that?"

Mike responded sarcastically, "Let me think and see if I can figure it out."

"Without a doubt he is a womanizer and is a regular in the barrooms and strip clubs of the city."

Paul had told James that the head of the state police told him that Donald had been arrested by the police numerous times for DUI. Finally the police chief told him that the next time, he would go to prison.

"Donald may be a really good man, but his addiction to women and drugs truly will destroy him," Mike said.

"From what I've learned about him, he could have been successful in any career path he chose."

"It seems that many lobbyists have addiction problems, mostly alcohol. However, Donald's is also drugs."

"Over and over again, I hear someone talking about a lobbyist who checked himself into a chemical dependency treatment center. There are so many opportunities to indulge in alcohol, we need to be careful, or we could become addicted to it."

"My God, I'm told by everyone there are so many parties during the legislative session that we need to attend," James said. "The parties are a way to get to know legislators and other lobbyists. All these events involve alcohol, but they are an excellent place to meet the people you need to know."

"One lobbyist told me that the organizations or lobbyists giving a party appreciate other lobbyists attending because it makes them look more connected," Mike said. "Both of us don't have to attend every party. We can swap the party duty."

CONCRETE, A MAJOR NEW CLIENT

James and Kimberly walked to the Cellar Bar from the capitol. Inside, the old German greeted them with a nod of his head.

"James, I have some more good information for you," Kimberly said. "This week the lobbyist for the State Concrete Association came by our office and announced he was retiring. He asked that we not tell anyone, but there are no secrets in the capitol. That means concrete will be hiring a new lobbyist."

James realized he had hit a gold mine with Kimberly. In a very short period of time, she had alerted him to several possible new clients.

Then the conversation again moved to more personal things, such as likes and dislikes and what to do during the week. After finishing her martini, Kimberly said, "I have to go. I can't drink anymore. I have a big day tomorrow with staff meetings and other things." James paid the tab and wished the old German farewell.

Outside, James asked Kimberly, "You think that old man is guilty of war crimes?"

"Absolutely, yes. He's probably hiding out here hoping he won't be found and prosecuted."

"You're right. He looks like the kind of guy who probably committed crimes of some sort. Did you notice he never smiles?"

"Yes, and he sounds so rough."

"You're right, but it was nice of him to go into the back room so we could talk privately. Plus, he makes a hell of a martini."

"Yes, I'd go back there. I like the place."

"Me too."

The tip Kimberly gave him about the concrete lobbyist's retiring could be good for GOB and Associates. Concrete could be another client. James was going to be right on it as soon as possible. The next morning he looked up the papers filed by the concrete lobbyist and found the name of the president of the association. James called Mr. Gonzalez and asked if he could meet with him. Mr. Gonzalez wanted to meet at lunch, but he couldn't meet with James for two weeks because he was going to be out of town. They said they would talk again when he returned. Meanwhile, James and Mike studied the concrete industry to determine what legislation would have an impact on it. Concrete could be very similar to the independent truckers they already represented.

James called Kimberly and asked her if she knew what bills would affect concrete producers. She said she would ask around and find out for him.

A day went by, and Kimberly called.

"People in the office tell me concrete has a problem with truck weight laws, environmental issues, law enforcement, and lien law bills that make certain the contractors pay their bills on time," she said. "The concrete lobbyist has to watch the contractors because they are always trying to amend laws to their advantage over their subcontractors." James couldn't thank her enough for being so helpful.

Then he said, "I can't wait to see you. Let's go by the old German's place tonight."

"OK, our usual time?"

"Yes, see you there."

James had not told Mike about his close relationship with Kimberly yet.

Kimberly and James met at the Cellar Bar at five o'clock. They had nicknamed it the Cell.

FACING THE REAL WORLD

A few days later Mike and James were soon facing the real world. It didn't always happen like it had with the building materials dealers and truckers. A very important linchpin client had refused to hire them. When James got back to the office, he called Kimberly and told her of his misfortune with Mr. Gonzales and concrete. Concrete would not hire GOB.

She said, "Who knows? He might reconsider later."

"There's no chance."

"You never know. Magic wands sometimes change things."

"Unfortunately, we don't have a magic wand." James sounded depressed.

When they got off the phone, Kimberly called her father. He owned one of the largest banks in the United States and several other businesses. He was listed in *Forbes* magazine as the fifteenth richest man in the world. He called the governor. The governor called the president of the State Concrete Association, Mr. Gonzalez.

A week later Mr. Gonzalez called James and Mike and said, "I have reconsidered. The State Concrete Association would like to have you boys represent them as their lobbyist. We will give you a five-year contract, but you must know that if the members become unhappy with your services, we will fire you." Then Mr. Gonzalez said, "Remember, boys, as long as you're winning, you're hired, but when you lose, you're fired. Your pay will be one hundred and twenty thousand per year for five years. We give bonuses for bills passed and no bonuses for the bills that we want killed."

James and Mike were shocked but happy. They thanked Mr. Gonzales and told him they understood. Now they had a megaclient, one that could carry a lot of influence because of all the independent producers across the state.

James immediately called Kimberly to tell her what had happened. She said, "That's great, James. I knew you were giving up too quickly. It must've been that magic wand you waved." Kimberly never told James how he got the job. "Are there any other groups you would like to represent?"

"Not at this time. We may have all we can handle in our first session."

The administration prefiled a truck weight bill lowering the number of yards a concrete truck could carry. The bill also affected independent truckers. The president of the State Concrete Association had mailed Mike a list of concrete companies in the state, but they needed to be put into a database. They searched the yellow pages and found Phyllis's Secretarial Services, and saw that she also did mailings.

After meeting with Phyllis, they hired her. Mike gave her the street addresses of the concrete companies to do the mailings. She was great. Within one day she had a mailing out to the concrete producers, and the GOB made a phone call to back it up telling them about the prefiled bill. The letter also stressed the importance of calling their legislators and objecting to the bill.

The GOB and Associates phones started ringing. Concrete producers called and told them they had talked to their state senators and representatives. They made notes. They could now start counting the votes on the committee. They were both absolutely amazed. They were now the "rhinestone cowboys" of concrete. As in the lyrics of the song, they were receiving phone calls, cards, and letters from people they didn't even know. They had become a part of an amazing grassroots organization.

Some of the concrete people wanted to know more about them, some just wanted to talk about the legislation, and others were ready to put up more money if needed. What a deal; they now wielded amazing political power through the grass roots of concrete producers and independent truckers. Legislators knew that anyone who could organize groups like truckers and concrete producers could also organize a campaign against them in the next election, so they had best listen to what Mike or James wanted. The last thing a legislator wanted was a letter or phone call from a lobbyist telling local people he was not voting their interest.

"If we get this reaction from all the groups, we will need a war room, a place to chart all of this, so we can track who knows who and who can pull whose string, who has the ability to sway a legislator to vote our way and who doesn't," Mike said. "I will create the war room. It will be on my back office wall."

One concrete producer suggested that James and Mike take the entire senate Transportation Committee out for a fine dinner so they could get to know them. The concrete producers had provided them with expense money for such occasions. They thought maybe they should do what the concrete producer suggested.

THE WAR ROOM

Mike went to the architectural store at the state university and purchased foam boards that had been divided into small squares. He covered almost the entire wall in his office with the boards. He listed the legislators on one side and the grassroots contacts on the top of each board. He created one board for each of the groups represented. Then he developed a code to explain who knew whom in the squares. All was very neatly printed and laid out.

James suggested he just record the data on the computer. Mike said he wanted the data to be more visual. He used the computer to statistically analyze the data and then recorded it on the wall. The more activity shown by an individual's name meant the more politically powerful he was, or at least it would show that person's level of political involvement. The charts also would reveal when an individual contacted a legislator and if the response given was positive or negative. In other words, did the legislator vote as the person asked, or did he ignore the request?

DO YOU HAVE INTENTIONS?

Back at the old German's bar, Kimberly said, "I can only have one drink, and then I'll have to go. I have another important meeting tomorrow. The legislative session is getting close, you know." Then she said, "But I want to go by your office. I bought you something for it."

"What did you buy?"

"It's in my purse. You will have to wait until we get to your office. I want to put it in the right place."

"I should be buying you things, you have been so helpful to me."

"Just a friend helping a friend."

"Let's drink fast because I can't wait to see what it is."

"OK, but on second thought, James, I need something to eat."

He asked the bartender if he had a menu they could see. The German brought an old, worn-out menu that obviously had not been reprinted in years. The prices had been changed many times.

James saw that he offered sauerkraut and sausage. "I have to try this. My mother was German, and she cooked sauerkraut and sausage once a week for us."

"I'll try it, but a small plate, please."

After eating they walked to James's office laughing and talking as always. He picked a small flower from a bush and gave it to her. James continuously tried to guess what was in her purse, but she would not tell him. He had to wait. At the office Kimberly took two neatly gift-wrapped packages out of her purse and told James to open them. He proceeded with his usual slow paper-saving procedure while Kimberly exclaimed, "Hurry up and open the packages!"

"Opening a package is like sex. It needs to go slow and easy," James quietly said.

"Is that all men think about?"

He laughed and continued to remove the paper slowly. The first package was two Monte Blanc pens, and the other was a sterling silver engraved name plaque to place on his desk.

"Kimberly, these are expensive gifts," James said.

"So what? I spend my money as I like, and I like spending it on you."

She took the name plaque out of his hand, placed it on the front center of his desk, and told him that was where it should be so visitors could easily read his name. James walked around his desk, put his arms around her, and hugged her tightly.

As they walked back to the capitol, Kimberly said she needed to go up to her office to retrieve some papers to go over that night for the meeting the next day.

James thought out loud, "Oh, a workaholic."

"No, I am not a workaholic, just a person who doesn't want to look unprepared."

Inside the capitol, Kimberly and James took the elevator to her office floor.

"Watch your behavior in the elevators. They have cameras. The other day they filmed a couple making love in this elevator," Kimberly said.

"What did they do about it?"

"Nothing, but the security officers showed the film to all of us in the office, and everyone had a good laugh."

"Are there any cameras in your office?"

"Why? Do you have intentions?"

"No, remember we're just friends. No sex."

James held the elevator door open while Kimberly ran into her office and picked up her briefcase and the papers she needed. Outside the capitol, Kimberly got in her car and James wished her good night. He put his head through the window and kissed her cheek. After a light but friendly laugh, Kimberly said, "You're getting a little personal there for friends, aren't you?"

"Oh, I'm sorry," he said.

"That was nice. Don't apologize," she said with a smile on her face.

On her drive home, she realized that every time she left James behind, she felt an emptiness in her heart. This was a feeling she'd never had before. She knew she had fallen in love with James, and she liked the feeling.

THE BANKERS

The next morning at their breakfast meeting, James told Mike he had attended a budget hearing last week. It was one of those budget hearings that took place during the interim in preparation for the next session and to oversee the state budget. He said that he and Bobby, the banker's lobbyist, had been sitting on a bench in the hallway outside the committee room. Bobby was complaining about a representative who had voted against him.

"I guess I'm going to have to put that son of a bitch on the board of directors of his local bank," Bobby had said. "Then we can pay him an outrageous fee for attending the one board meeting per month. That will put the bastard in our pocket, and he will have to vote for us, or we will kick his ass off the board, and he will not get any pay."

Bobby had looked at James and said, "What a great system. The only problem is we don't have enough board positions to put all the bullshitters on one."

A few days later, James had run across Bobby and asked him how it was going with the representative.

"Oh, we put the son of a bitch on the board, and he's with us now. Next year we're going to get the governor to take him off the Banking Committee. Then we will boot him off the board of the bank and try to defeat the son of a bitch in the next election. He has been a pain in the ass. He stepped over the line that bankers will tolerate. Can you believe he tried to reduce the interest rate on commercial loans to a maximum of eight percent rather than the favorable percentage we get now? Hell, you know the usury law allows thirty-six percent, and we could charge that on personal loans. He tried to reduce usury to twelve percent!

"We will teach him a lesson in the next election. He just hasn't felt the heat yet. Wait till we call his loans at the bank. That reminds me, I'm going to tell them at the bank not to loan him any more money. That way we can really get his ratty ass in a bind. He thinks he's on the gravy train, but I'll show him."

After he finished telling Mike the story, James said, "As Bobby walked away, I scratched my head thinking, is this really happening?"

"Everything seems to be connected. There's a loophole that leads to money everywhere," Mike said.

THEATERS AND THE DANCE BEGINS

At one of their meetings at the Cellar Bar, Kimberly asked James if he had had any luck getting new clients. He told her they had a planned meeting with a little theater manager.

"Brian, a young grad student, had provided the contact information of the theater manager. We met Brian at the Capitol House Bar. He is working on his PhD in political science," James said.

Kimberly said, "A little theater manager! Why would they need a lobbyist?"

"He wants to do something with a special tax to promote little theaters."

"Interesting. There is some legal precedent for that."

"What do you mean, legal precedent?"

"The libraries have a special tax. It's added to everyone's property tax. It's a very small percentage. That tax is the reason the libraries in the state are so modern and up-to-date. Look at a property tax bill, and you will see it listed."

"That's good information," James said. "That's probably what he wants for little theaters. I owe you big-time."

"No, James, I'm just helping a friend."

The GOB met the theater manager at one of the city's upscale restaurants. He told them he wanted to pass a tax that would help the theaters. James told him there was precedence for such a tax because the libraries had gotten a portion of all property taxes collected statewide. Mike wondered where James had gotten this information. He didn't realize Kimberly was feeding it to him. The theater manager was aware of the library tax.

The manager said, "What would you boys charge us to pass such a bill?"

"How much are you willing to pay?" Mike asked. "I would have to raise the money, but I feel certain I can raise forty thousand dollars to start, and if you pass a bill, I can raise another forty thousand dollars."

"Will you give us three sessions to pass the bill?" James asked. "During the first session, we will learn where the opposition is. In the next two sessions, we will bury them. It took the library lobbyist three sessions to pass their bill."

Again, Mike was wondering where the hell James was getting this information. He would ask him later.

The manager said, "OK, let me start raising the money today. I will let you know how I'm doing in two weeks."

"Great, we look forward to hearing from you," James said.

Two weeks later the theater manager called and said he had raised the forty thousand. They now had another legitimate paying client.

Two days later James and Kimberly met at Jack's Bistro for dinner. Kimberly told James she would like to go by his office again. In his office Kimberly told James to sit behind the desk and close his eyes. He did as he was told. She took a gift-wrapped package out of her purse and placed it on the desk.

Then she said, "Open your eyes."

He opened them and looked at the package. "What is this?"

"Just open it and see." He slowly unwrapped the paper from the package. Inside the box was a nice silver letter opener with "Good Ole Boys & Associates" engraved on the handle.

"How nice of you. It's beautiful! I love it! I will think of you every time I use it."

He walked around the desk to her; she was already standing. He stood close to her, and they looked at each other as if they wanted to kiss, but knew better. The urge to kiss was too strong, and their lips collided. They kissed like teenagers wildly in love. Their relationship had changed forever.

"Oh, we should not have done that," James said.

"You're right," she said. Then they kissed again. She had never experienced so strong a desire as she felt for James. "We need to think about this before we go too far. Would you like to go sit on the capitol steps?"

"Yes, that's a good idea."

While sitting on the steps, James told Kimberly about a lobbyist who had warned him about becoming a drunk. The legislative parties had started. Associations gave parties every night. Lobbyists gave parties to entertain the legislature and influence votes. Members of the associations would go to the parties and mingle with the legislators. There was always a plentiful amount of food available for everyone. Alcohol flowed freely. Many lobbyists and legislative staffers attended the parties because there was free food every night, or at least when the legislature was in session. The secretary who coordinated them invited Mike and James to all the parties, or they would just follow the others after adjournment. During legislative sessions these parties were almost every night of the week. Lobbyists were expected to attend whether they received an invitation or not.

"At a legislative party last week, after a Budget Committee hearing, a lobbyist told me he was going to show me how not to become an alcoholic," James said.

"We were standing to the side of the room, but where most at the party could see us. He had a wine glass in his hand with a small amount of wine remaining in it. He quietly but intentionally dropped it on the concrete floor. The glass shattered, and the red wine splattered across the floor. I was shocked and amazed at what he had done. He immediately apologized and asked for a broom or mop so he could clean up the mess he had made. I assumed, and was correct, that no one in the room knew he had done it intentionally. He was such a gentleman, apologetic and helpful in cleaning up.

"After all the commotion, he looked at me and quietly said, 'We can now ease out the back door. They have all seen us. They all know that we were at the party. In a few weeks they will remember just us, not the wine glass dropping.'

"He told me the longer you remain at the parties, the more likely you are to drink, and the more you drink, the more likely you are to become an alcoholic. The only purpose of going to the parties is to be seen and to gather information, which can also be gathered during the regular legislative day.

"At the next party, he told me to follow him and to do what he did. He walked around the room shaking hands with everyone, greeting them with a smile, and discussing subjects they might want to discuss. After making the complete round of the room, he said, 'See the door to the kitchen?' I said yes. 'They've all seen us, so now we can leave.'"

Kimberly said, "You got some good advice from this man. All you need to do is be seen and leave. He is right: many lobbyists become drunks." They talked for more than two hours, never mentioning the kiss. As Kimberly's taillights again faded away into the night, James thought, *What just happened? Did she kiss me or did I kiss her?* He had never felt a woman's touch so strongly. Something about her was different than any woman he had ever met.

Later the same week, during a phone conversation, James asked Kimberly if she would like to get together again. She said she was playing volleyball after work that week, but she would be free for lunch any day. James thought lunch was a great idea and asked her where she would like to go.

"Let me think about it, and I will call you back," Kimberly said. "No, I won't have to call you back. I live close by, and there is a little café named Luna near my condo that needs the business. After lunch I could show you my place, if you'd like to see it. Let me be clear, no sex."

"I agree. What's the address? I will meet you there."

"The address is 666 Nederland Street. Remember James, that's six, six, six, not sex, sex, sex."

James laughed. "I will put the address in my GPS. See you there at twelve thirty tomorrow."

He couldn't wait for the next day. He was looking forward to seeing her again. The invitation to see her condo would give him a better insight into her and how she lived. He wanted to know more about her, what kind of woman she was. At twelve thirty James arrived at the little restaurant a few minutes ahead of Kimberly. There were few people in the restaurant.

They had a fast lunch and went to Kimberly's condo around the corner. It was immaculate, wonderfully decorated, and could've been in *Architectural Digest* magazine. Kimberly clearly was a woman of good and expensive tastes. James wondered how she could afford such a luxurious condo on a state employee salary, but he did not ask.

Kimberly hadn't told James the whole story. She was from a very rich and powerful political family. The state job was nothing more than to have something to do. Kimberly had already been given her first billion—that's billion with a *B*—but she was not telling James. As they walked through the large condo, James couldn't believe his eyes.

"I bought this place at a bargain price. The people who owned it needed the money and surprised me when they took my lowball offer. I expected them to ask for more," Kimberly said.

When they got to Kimberly's bedroom, James was surprised by its size. It was huge. She had a king-size bed in it, and there was room for another one.

James lay down on the bed and said, "This condo is so big. I'm tired of walking."

"Get off the bed. There's not going to be any sex," Kimberly said. James agreed.

She put her hand out to help him get up, but he pulled slightly, and she fell on the bed beside him. It was not from his pulling. It was like a fall she wanted to make. She just needed to appear reluctant, and she did.

They kissed passionately. He rolled over on top of her, and she pulled him close. She could feel his erection against her body. Their passion was so hot that the room was heating. He unbuttoned her blouse, and she unbuttoned his shirt. They did everything except tear each other's clothes off.

"Stop," she said. "To do this you have to love me."

"Kimberly, you know that I care for you." She didn't seem to notice that he did not say *love*, but used the word *care*. "I am not into one-night stands."

"Nor am I," she said.

She submitted to his obvious wishes. Their love was so passionate. It was as if neither had ever had sex before.

When it was over, James whispered, "Kimberly, you're even more beautiful nude. You have a perfect body."

James was confused. He was uncertain as to whether it was love or just lust. Something about Kimberly was truly different from other women he had known. Whatever it was, it was wonderful. She seemed to have touched the bottom of his soul, a place where no other woman had ever been.

"I have a gift for you, James."

"Another gift? You've given me almost everything I will ever need in life."

"I don't think so. There are a few other things you may be missing. Be a good boy and open the gift."

James opened the gift in his usual slow-motion way, as if he were saving the paper to be used again. That always flustered Kimberly because she wanted him to tear open the package. She was like a little kid with no patience, waiting to see his expression when the gift was revealed. Inside the package was a beautiful pair of cordovan wingtip shoes.

James was surprised and said, "They're my size. How did you know?"

"I looked in another pair of your shoes at your office."

James examined the shoes and noted, "They are from Saks Fifth Avenue. They must have cost a fortune. How can you do all this on a state employee's salary?"

"I'm frugal."

"You must be." He put the shoes on and walked around looking at them.

"You're a beautiful man, and I love you very much. You're the man I have been looking for all my life."

James gently kissed her on her cheek and said, "Thank you very much for the shoes, but we must get back to work. I just wish I could be as giving and loving as you."

"Don't worry; you will be, because I will teach you. I hope I have a lifetime to do just that."

CHAPTER 4

WARP SPEED AHEAD, MR. SPEAKER

SESSION BEGINS

The first day of the session, the capitol was as active as bees on a beehive. The coffee shop, which usually had no more than five or ten people in it at a time, was now packed with people. The security guards at the door had been doubled. There was a waiting line to get in for coffee. The buffet food line opened early and planned to stay open late.

James and Mike didn't know who was whom—who was a senator or representative, who were the lobbyists, or who were just people from the general public. The shoe-shine stand was full. People were walking with briefcases and papers in their hands. There were more pretty young women than they could believe. Almost everyone wore a coat and tie. Overnight the capitol had truly changed. It had gone from a laid-back and basically empty building to an overactive office building packed with people.

Donald calmly maintained his usual coffee table. People came back to greet him as if he were the man of the day. Mike and James sat at the table with Donald, and he introduced them to several other lobbyists. Donald seemed to know everyone. They met lobbyists for energy, chemicals, Fortune 500s, hairdressers, mental health workers, automobile dealers, and other businesses. The big elephants in the room seemed to be the head of labor and the leader of business and industry. Everyone wanted to talk to them.

Television cameras were everywhere, with interviews taking place in every corner. The big event of the day was scheduled for noon, when the governor would open the session with a speech.

Donald said, "It's always fun to get a seat in the gallery to watch and listen to the speech, but it's mostly unimportant to guys like you and me. He will be talking about bigger issues than we will be concerned about or get involved with during the session."

FINANCIAL PLANNING

The firm was on its way to being a force to be dealt with in state politics. Neither Mike nor James could believe they had put all this together so easily. They had more money in the bank than either one ever imagined making and so quickly. They represented some major state and locally owned companies. With the right kind of grassroots organizational effort, they could be politically significant. But neither had ever worked with a grassroots organization.

They had more than three hundred thousand dollars in the bank. James wanted to invest the money they were not using in the stock market, but Mike, the more conservative one, said no. James pointed out that he could invest on the margin and double the money. Mike thought that was too risky. They agreed to put three hundred thousand dollars in a money market fund.

Mike suggested to James that they take the same salary they were making at their previous jobs, because they may need money in the future, in case they lost a client. The possibility of losing a client was high, because neither one of them knew much about politics. They had been allotted several thousand dollars in expenses, in addition to the more than three hundred thousand dollars they had in the bank. They decided they would complete expense reports and take the money from those clients who provided entertainment funds.

Mike pointed out that the CPA said he needed to formalize the method they used to take funds for entertainment.

James asked, "Can I take funds out of the corporation for entertaining lady friends?"

Mike laughed and said, "Absolutely yes, if she's a benefit to our business. And of course I would do the same thing for Catherine occasionally. She deserves some entertainment for supporting me while getting into this crazy business."

"No problem. I agree."

"I will write the checks, and both of us will sign them," Mike said.

"Sounds like a plan that will work for me," James said.

"OK, we will do it."

FACIAL RECOGNITION

"James, did you meet Todd, the guy with the beer retailers?" Mike asked. "He has been lobbying for years, and he's amazing. His power in the legislature was unbelievable. Paul told me that years ago, he kept the drinking age from increasing from eighteen to twenty-one. He persuaded a committee to reject federal highway funds to keep the feds from forcing the state to increase the legal drinking age. This would have caused the state to lose millions of dollars in highway construction funds."

"How did he do it?" James asked.

"He's smart and works hard. He has a large group of bar owners and rich beer wholesalers as grassroots supporters, not to mention the incredible amount of money the Beer Association spends on electing candidates. Most important of all, he has been the lobbyist for the group for years, and legislators know and trust him. Like other powerful lobbyists, his face is recognizable by legislators, and he has not been associated with any controversy. Legislators may not know your name, but they know your face. He abides by the old philosophy, 'See no evil, hear no evil, and speak no evil.' He only gets involved with legislation that has to do with the sale of beer."

"There is a party almost every night at the Beer Association office during the legislative session," James said. "When the legislature is not in session and a committee is meeting, his office had an open house. There are drinks, food, and entertainment. It is a gathering place for all those involved in legislation. Everyone, including lobbyists, legislative staffers, and legislators, are invited. Someone told me legislative staffers who wanted a free meal went to his nightly events. He stayed in his office, and all the peons walked by to say, 'Thank you, sir.' This man is good at what he does, and whether you agree with his legislative activities or not, you have to respect him."

"Yes, he is hired to represent a legal business and does what they expect," Mike said.

THEATER BILLS TO BE INTRODUCED

The theater group had managed to get two senators to agree to author and introduce their bill. The bill number would later be SB2065. SB stands for a senate bill, and HB identifies a house bill. Theater managers did not have a list of theaters throughout the state. Because they didn't have a contact list, James and Mike had a problem. Such a list would be needed to develop a grassroots group.

James called his newest friend, Donald, and asked him what to do.

"Develop your own," Donald said. "Look in the yellow pages for a list, buy a list from a list seller, or hire someone to contact all the chambers of commerce and the arts organizations."

"What is a list seller?" James asked.

"A list seller is a company that develops lists and sells them to people for advertising purposes."

"Thank you, Donald. I hope to see you in the coffee shop soon, and I'm buying the coffee."

Mike found a list seller. He bought a list of little theaters in the state.

Mike told James, "This list has turned out to be a piece of shit, a piece of shit at a high price. I'm working with the CPA, and we both are answering concrete and trucker calls. We need to spend more time at the capitol to get to know people and what's going on over there."

"Let me talk to someone at the capitol to see if she can tell me how other lobbyists manage," James said. "Let me make the call real quick."

James called Kimberly and started the conversation with, "My God, this is really getting to be work."

"You can handle it," she said.

James, in a low tone, replied immediately, "I'd like to handle you right now."

"Maybe later, sweetheart."

"Can you tell me how lobbyists handle mailings, researching addresses, and other secretarial duties?"

"Hire someone to do it," she said. "University students are less expensive. That's what the legislative staff does during the legislative session. The students are smart and computer literate and can do more than you would expect."

"That's a great idea. I'm on it. Thank you. Bye. I'll talk to you later."

Quickly, before he could get off the line, she said, "Hold on, boy, information like that deserves a martini at the Cellar Bar."

"Sure, five o'clock?"

"No, I have to work late today. Is seven thirty OK?"

"Yes. See you there at seven thirty."

James then went to Mike's office and said, "A university student—that's the answer. I understand the university pays them minimum wage. If we add a dollar or two to the minimum wage, we can hire the best."

"If we offer one dollar per hour more than the university, they'll be standing in line to work for us," Mike said.

He was right. A notice on the university bulletin board produced several applicants for the job. They hired a young lady named Nan, who had extremely good computer skills. Within a week she had developed a comprehensive list of theaters throughout the state. They turned the list over to Phyllis with a letter to be sent to all. The next day Phyllis had it in the mail.

Again, the phones started ringing, but this time it was a different kind of call. Most of the calls were from people telling Mike and James what a great idea it was for the theaters, but they had not talked to their representative or senator. Most of them did not know their representative or senator or anyone else associated with legislation. This was a very weak political group. That meant the GOB was on its own.

This was a problem because they did not know most of the senators and representatives, much less have the ability to get them to vote. What could they do? Those who put up the forty thousand dollars must know something about legislation.

They contacted Bruce with the theater group and asked him who the contributors were and if he could get them together. To their surprise it was not the theater managers who had made the contributions. It was rich supporters of the theaters.

After discussing the problem with Bruce, they came up with an idea. They would develop a list of rich contributors who could influence the legislature. They managed to get Bruce to sign off on a letter to all the theater managers asking them for a list of the patrons who might help. This time the response was different. Phones started ringing again. Before they knew it, they had a list of more than twenty-five people who had contributed more than twenty thousand dollars to a little theater.

Next, a second letter went out to the more than twenty-five patrons, asking them to contact their legislators and report back to the GOB their response. Phones rang even more. By the end of the week, five other senators had signed on as cosponsors of the bill.

James said to Mike, "Remember, it's all about money, and it was. Money talked."

During one of their conversations, James asked Mike, "Do you realize that we are developing an unbelievable network of wealthy people who have power over legislation?"

"Yes, there's no limit to what we could do with these lists."

"Yes, run you for state senate."

Mike hesitated for a moment and said, "Let's not talk like that, because the last thing a legislator wants to do is support potential opposition candidates. We need to concentrate on GOB and Associates. James, you would make a better candidate. You understand television, you're nice looking, and you have a voice made for broadcasting." James laughed but did not comment.

The next day Mike and James really went to work doing what Donald had suggested, such as getting ready to send letters. The letters had to be printed at Kinko's because they did not have a copy machine. Then the letters had to be put into GOB and Associates Incorporated envelopes, which they did not have, and then they had to be addressed.

"This is goddamn work," Mike said. "I never expected to have to do all this fucking mailing. I thought all we had to do was bullshit a few bullshitters.

THE APARTMENT DOWNTOWN

"We are spending a lot of time downtown, and the round trip to our homes is more than seventy miles each day. Also, we're going to be here late at night several nights a week."

Mike, the loving husband he was, spoke aggressively. "I'm going home at night, no matter how late it is. You're on your own when it comes to an apartment."

"OK, I'll get a cheap place, a two-bedroom in case you change your mind."

"No, I'm not going to change my mind. Rent a one-bedroom. They're less expensive."

James called Kimberly and told her he was going to rent an apartment downtown.

She said, "That's wonderful; we can spend more time together. You could stay with me."

"I don't think that's a good idea," James said.

"Maybe you're right, but if you change your mind, you can have my second bedroom. I only use it when my mother and father want to spend the night with me, and that's not very often."

"Thanks, but that could get complicated. Have you ever lived with a man before?"

"No, and I have never wanted to live with one until now. You should get a short-term or month-to-month lease because you might change your mind. You don't snore, do you?"

"No."

James asked Kimberly to ask the state employees in her office if any of them knew of an inexpensive apartment nearby.

She said yes, she would do it that day. She would make certain it was close to the state capitol, her condo, and his office, but not too close to his office, since it was not in the best neighborhood.

Two hours later Kimberly called and said, "I have found a place for you. It's not fancy, but it's a two-bedroom and rents for only five hundred per month. It also is a month-to-month lease. Let's go look at it today after work."

"OK, I can do that anytime after four," James said.

After work James and Kimberly met at the apartment address. An elderly lady came to the door.

James asked, "Do you have an apartment for rent?"

She said, "Yes, you have the right place. It is a garage apartment in the back. I would give it to you free, because I need someone who looks like you to be there just for safety, but my son insists that I collect rent. I can't advertise because we get people we don't want on the property wanting to rent it."

"Could we look at it, please?"

"Yes, let me get the key."

They walked about fifty feet to the garage and went up the stairs on the left side. The elderly lady unlocked the door. It was a cute little apartment with bedroom, one bath, a living room, and a small kitchen.

"Are you going to take the apartment?" Kimberly asked.

"Yes, I will take it." He offered to give the lady money for the first month's rent. "Could we start the rent on the first day of the month?" he asked.

"Yes, that's not a problem." The first day of the month was when the session started.

James had only four hundred dollars in his wallet, so Kimberly added the other hundred. No signed lease was required.

They thanked her, and she gave them the key. They walked down the street on the way to Kimberly's office laughing and talking about how nice it was going to be having a place so perfectly located. James told Kimberly he would repay her the one hundred dollars she had loaned him.

Kimberly said, "That's no problem. Don't worry about it."

"Oh no, I will pay you."

Upon returning to his office, Mike said, "James, how about dinner with the wives again?"

James confessed, "Mike, I haven't been completely straight with you. Sarah and I agreed to separate last year."

"But you were at dinner with my wife and me, and we thought you were happily married!"

"We're still good friends and do things together."

"What happened?"

"Nothing, and there was no third party involved when we separated. We just wanted to go our own ways."

"Well, Catherine is not going to believe this, but it's wonderful that you're still good friends and enjoy each other's company."

"That's true. Neither of us could see any benefit from fighting and destroying each other's name and reputation. Also, I have not told you that I rented an apartment downtown. It is very inexpensive, a hole-in-the-wall kind of place, which works out perfectly for the office location. I will rarely need to use my car."

"I hope everything works out with you and your wife, but if it doesn't, I understand. Things change in life, don't they?"

"Yes, they do."

Later that week James took his wife to dinner, and they decided to finalize their divorce amicably. They both hoped to continue their peaceful and friendly relationship for the rest of their lives.

THE FIRST WEEK

Few bills were being heard the first week, so James and Mike wandered the capitol the entire week. They met and talked to numerous lobbyists. They were building a network they could use in the future.

James went back to the office and told Mike about a lobbyist he had met that day. The lobbyist spoke so softly that James didn't get his name, but he gave James some advice about using the phone and the press. He told him he had been a lobbyist for more than fifteen years. He certainly had been around. He represented the mental health workers. He was older and didn't look like he was in good health. He also had one or two individuals he represented. He seemed like a nice guy, and his stories were sort of fascinating.

The elderly lobbyist told James, "There are always rumors about someone being investigated around the state capitol. After you have been around a few years, you will learn that most of the time, the rumors were started by someone's political enemy or opposition. Certainly at some point, all lobbyists are likely to be recorded by the FBI. Not because they did anything wrong, but just because they happened to call the person who was being investigated. In other words, say the governor was being investigated, and I called to talk to the governor.

"My good lawyer friend Craig had the most creative way of ending a conversation that might be recorded and misinterpreted. When he had a conversation and discussed what might be going on that could possibly be a crime, he would end the conversation by saying, 'You know I have Jimmy Hoffa buried in my backyard. As you know, the FBI has been looking for his remains for years and is unable to find them. That's because I buried that son of a bitch six feet deep. It took days to dig the damn hole. Don't you tell anyone because they will have backhoes in my fucking backyard digging for him.'"

James continued the story, saying, "He said Craig would laugh and say that anyone who heard him talk about Jimmy Hoffa certainly thought he was crazy, and the authorities knew that things mentioned in the conversation were certainly said by a mentally insane son of a bitch and may not be admissible in any court. Then Craig would end the conversation by saying, 'I'll almost swear to everything I've said in this conversation.'"

"Most of us lobbyists will never become involved in a crime, because we are the good guys, you know," the old lobbyist had told James with a laugh. "What I just told you was just fun and games, but be careful what you say on the telephone, because you never know when it might become serious. My brother went to jail because of a conversation he thought was innocent."

The legislative staff was drafting bills by the thousands. Kimberly told James her office drafted more than four thousand bills. The legislative agenda was going to be difficult. There were many bills to hear in a short period of time. The legislative session only lasted sixty days.

"We need to get one of the legislators or a staffer to give us the code to the bills so we can read them online," Mike said. "What we're doing now, looking at the topics, then going to pay for a printed copy, is not only expensive, but we also might miss something because the bill title may not match the content. If we can't get a legislator to give us a code, maybe we can buy a digital service. Someone told me there might be such a bill-tracking service. You provide them the bill number, and they let you know when any movement takes place on the bill."

"That would be great," James said.

"Can you talk to your female friend at the capitol and see if she can help? Are you still talking to her?"

"Yes, several times when I need to have a question answered. I'll call her today."

Later James called Kimberly and asked if she would like to meet him at the Nazi's place.

"No, but I will meet you at my condo. Then I will have to come back to the office because the workload up here at the state capitol is just incredible these days. You know, all the last-minute bill drafting. Could you meet me at four?"

"Yes, I'll see you there." James arrived at Kimberly's condo at 3:50 p.m. Kimberly was five minutes late.

"I think your neighbors thought I was a pervert standing outside your door for so long."

"Here's a key. You can let yourself in, and my neighbors won't call the police."

"No, I don't want a key to your house."

"I insist."

Once inside, Kimberly and James grabbed at each other and started kissing passionately until they fell to the floor on the carpet. Kimberly took off her blouse, James removed her bra, and she ripped off his shirt. A button bounced across the carpet. They made passionate love. Afterward, they lay on the carpet looking at the chandelier in the foyer next to the living room where they were.

"We didn't make it to the bedroom," James said.

Kimberly said, "My God, no, we didn't. That was so wonderful. I wish I didn't have to go back to work. We could make love all afternoon."

They got up from the floor and put on their clothes.

"How am I going to explain the missing button?"

"Tell them you caught it on a door or something. We're not the only ones who have left work and made love. All of them have likely done the same thing with someone at one time or another. If they notice your button missing, they won't ask why; they will just assume you were misbehaving. They won't say anything. Don't worry about it."

NOT WHAT THE GOB THOUGHT IT WAS

During the first week of the session, a large number of bills were introduced, and the GOB had to read them all. Reviewing the bills became a time-consuming task. James and Mike divided the bills in half, and each took responsibility for reading his share of the bills. Bills ranged from neutering cats to naming buildings.

Legislators introduced many bills, sometimes at the request of just one constituent. The representative who introduced the bill knew it was going to fail before he filed it. Reading these bills took up James and Mike's time, but they had to read them word for word. Missing a word could cost the GOB a client. It was almost like going into hibernation for a week, because just one bill could affect one of their clients. So it was very important that the boys read every one of these bills to make certain their clients were not affected by one of them. Plus, one of them had to be at the legislature every day to make certain no amendments were introduced to any bills that would negatively affect one of their groups.

James announced to Mike, "This is work."

"You're right, James. This is more than just bullshitting bullshitters. It's serious. Some of these bills can change a person's entire life, and most of the public has no idea these bills have been introduced."

"Some of the bills can affect your relationship with your wife, your pocketbook, your church, your doctor, and so on."

"If the public knew about all these bills, they would want to reduce the legislative session to no more than two weeks a year to prevent them from being heard, much less becoming law. It's that old saying again, 'No man's wallet is safe when the legislature is in session.'"

"That's the damn truth," James responded.

In order to have peace and quiet so they could read the bills, they turned off their phones. The weather was beautiful. Spring flowers were blooming, and the trees were sporting beautiful green leaves. James found a picnic table on the capitol grounds where he could read without being disturbed. Mike preferred to stay in his office. He put a "Do Not Disturb" sign he had taken from the Capitol House Hotel on his door.

They only took a short break for lunch.

During lunch Mike said to James, "I never realized there were so many bullshit bills introduced into the state legislature. My God, all this bullshit is a waste of taxpayers' money and time."

James agreed. "I suppose some of the bills are filed to keep the legislator's hometown Indians from going on the warpath. The legislator who introduced the bill can go back home and say he tried to pass a bill to do this or that, but it was killed in the legislature. The clientele will be happy and put down their bows and arrows. I think this is what makes the polls show that the voters love their legislator and hate the legislature. The public has such little understanding of the legislative process that they think the legislator did something for them. Especially when he tells them the bill number he introduced."

"This has been a real learning experience," Mike said. "Shit, there was one bill defining fornication. What in the fuck was that all about?" They both laughed.

The theater bill had been introduced at the request of one of the theater managers. Theater managers had gotten two senators to cosign a bill. There were no bills introduced that would threaten the building materials dealers. The truck weights bill was found as expected.

WELCOME TO THE HARDBALL SPORT

Back at the Capitol House Bar, James and Mike were trying to make new friends, get the latest scoop, have a cocktail or two, and discuss the activities of the day. Old Senator

Jackson called the boys to his booth, where he was sitting with the whore of the day.

"I understand you boys are doing great and that you have managed to get some interesting clients."

Mike replied, "Yes, Senator, that's correct.

"How many clients do you have now?" the senator asked,

"Four," Mike said.

"That's not bad," said the senator.

The senator started giving Mike and James some advice. "You boys need to understand that politics is a hardball sport. I guess you're sure you're ready to play. Beware that some injuries last a lifetime.

"When I pointed out to one business lobbyist that the hazardous waste bill he was pushing would cause the death of many people, he said, 'A little hazardous waste never hurt anyone.' Can you boys think like that? Can you focus on your clients' interest above all else, no matter how much you disagree personally? Can you mislead someone by omission with a smile on your face? Can you convince yourself that good government is whatever is good for your clients first and the public second? Personally, years ago when I was a foolish young man, it was very difficult for me to adjust to the rules of the game. With all that said, I think you will find that most lobbyists are good people despite what the public thinks. Welcome to the sport, boys."

"I would like to invite you boys to a poker game in my penthouse suite." The old senator said, "I can't invite you tonight because I have a full table, but how about tomorrow night? The game starts at eight. You do play poker, don't you?"

"Yes, Senator, we will be there. Thanks for the invitation."

"Both of you, right?" he asked.

"Yes," they replied.

"OK, I'll see you boys tomorrow night, but you need to move on now, because me and this beautiful young lady have some business to transact. You know, some of that private kind of business."

The next day when James was talking to Kimberly, he told her about the old senator's invitation.

"Oh, you're in the big time now," He said. "Let me tell you how it works. You are expected to lose five hundred dollars each to the senator. Then, no matter how late you stay, make certain you don't win it back. Losing the five hundred dollars each doesn't mean he's going to do anything to help you. It simply means he's not going to hurt you. If you need help, you're going to have to lose a lot more."

"Damn, this could get expensive," James said.

"Yes, but it's more expensive if you don't play the game."

CHAPTER 5

FRUGAL CAN RESULT IN GENIUS

WINING AND DINING CAN BE EXPENSIVE

From what James and Mike could gather, it appeared that the truck weight bill was going to be heard in committee during the first half of the session, and the governor's staff was going to push for its passage.

"Maybe we should take all the committee members out to dinner as one of the producers suggested," Mike said. "That way they will all know us when we come before the committee."

"That's a good idea, Mike. I'll set it up," James volunteered.

"Let's splurge on this and do it at the finest restaurant in town."

"I'm on it."

That afternoon James had an invitation printed inviting all the members of the Transportation Committee to dinner at the finest restaurant in town. The next Tuesday all the committee members showed up at seven o'clock as requested at the restaurant with their wives or a significant other. There were twenty-two of them. Wine was served before dinner in a private room. Each member ordered from the menu. This was a big mistake for James and Mike, because almost all ordered the most expensive items on the menu.

One young and arrogant member who had just been elected to the senate ordered a seventy-five-dollar bottle of wine for almost everyone at the dinner. It was a joyful event, and all the committee members enjoyed meeting the new lobbyists for the trucking industries. At the end of the evening, all the committee members thanked Mike and James as they departed. The bill was shocking. It was several thousand dollars for the night.

THE GREENHOUSE IS CREATED

The next morning the CPA came by the GOB office. James and Mike told him about the night. The CPA calculated that they were not making enough money to do that often.

"You could feed the entire legislature lunch in your office every day of the session for a little more money," he said. "Food is cheap."

A light bulb went off in both James's and Mike's heads.

"Yes, we could update and improve our small kitchen and hire a part-time cook during the day," James said. "Then invite only those who support us. The word would get out that you could get a free lunch if you supported GOB and Associates."

The CPA advised them to use it as a write-off. He said to keep records of who attended and what was discussed during the lunch. He said it was unbelievable what people will do for a free lunch.

The next day James called a contractor friend, and within a week, they had a commercial stove and a nice refrigerator in the large front room of their office. Mike found a cook who could work three or more hours each day for a fairly low wage.

James invited five of the Transportation Committee members to lunch at the office, which they referred to as the Greenhouse. Four of them accepted. The short walk to the office was easy for the legislators. They all enjoyed the lunch, and the cook was excellent. From James and Mike's point of view, it was much more productive because it was up close and personal. Compared to the outrageously expensive dinner at the finest restaurant in town, this was a cheap form of entertainment. They did not have to serve steak and lobster, just a simple lunch. Sometimes sandwiches would do. A smartass, one-term young state senator could not order seventy-five-dollar wine for everyone.

James told the four committee members to invite anyone they would like. Lunch would be served every day when the legislature was in session. The word spread rapidly. Legislators started coming ten or fifteen at a time. James and Mike had to buy more tables and chairs. They had suddenly become the most popular lobbyists in the legislature. They had hit a vote-getter gold mine.

The CPA estimated the cost at about thirty-five thousand dollars for the session. This was a good deal for the boys. They did not have to spend money buying expensive drinks and dinners at restaurants and bars anymore. At Kimberly's suggestion, James invited a few legislative staffers. Only those who were important to the GOB would be invited—those staffers who controlled when bills were heard and who were friendly to GOB. Kimberly made a list for James but did not include herself. She wanted to continue her low-profile relationship with James.

KILLING BILLS

"The truck weight law bills we should be worried about are numbers HB1456 and SB806," James said, thinking out loud. "I have read both bills, and we must kill both of them. The lobbyist named Donald was very open to answering questions for me. I think he could be helpful. I'm going to find him and question him as to how we can kill the bills and what we should do. He gave me his card. I'll call him and offer to buy him a cup of coffee. Maybe he will help us."

At the office, James called Donald and asked him if he was going to be in the coffee shop the next morning. Donald said he would be there at nine o'clock as always. James told him he would like to come by and talk to him. He said for James to come on by, that he was always welcome. The next morning James went to the coffee shop, and Donald was there, as always.

After the usual morning greetings, Donald said, "How can I help you?"

"I'm going to be straightforward with you. We don't know what the fuck we're doing, and we have clients depending on us. Please tell me how you kill a bill."

"OK, get your pencil and take notes." Donald said. "This is how I do it. First, you must rally the constituents. Send a letter to all of them and tell them to call their senator and representatives. Tell them a bill has been filed in the legislature that could negatively affect their business. Provide them the bill numbers."

"We have already done that," James said.

"Good. The next step is to send more postcards and letters. The more you send the better.

"In your letters, give them a list of talking points, such as the following: the cost of labor will go up, and consumers will have to pay more for the products. Provide the names and phone numbers of the senators and representatives on the committees who will hear the bills. Make it sound like the bills are going to cost them a lot of money. Ask them to call you to talk about the bills. Make notes of those who call you. Those who call you are the ones who will help you.

"Now, the phones should start ringing." Donald shrugged his shoulders and continued, "At least you hope they will. Tell them their call is important. For every phone call, a legislator knows that fifty people in his or her district are interested in the issue. Most keep notes of the phone calls to review before they vote.

"Keep reminding your clients to contact all senators and representatives weekly. Ask them to report to you what they and the senators and representatives talked about. Keep a running tally so that you will know what the vote is going to be before the testimony.

"Now that the legislators have received phone calls from their local voters, it's time for you to visit. Talk in person, not by phone, with every legislator on the committee who will hear your bills. You should know how they're going to vote before the committee meeting starts. You will win, if you don't get one of those good government bastards after you. Sometimes you have to lose a battle to win the war. If your bill gets to the house or senate floor, good luck, because you will have to deal with all the members of the chamber. You're going to have to work your ass off."

Donald made it sound so simple. James and Mike were not certain it was that easy. At least now they had a plan of action. Visiting with all the committee members was going to be time-consuming.

THE BROOM CLOSET

Later Donald said, "Mike, you and James need to walk the committee room halls and look at the posted notices on the hearing rooms. If one of your bills is listed for hearing this week, it will be on the notice. If your bill or bills are posted you need to bust your ass to get ready for the hearing. That's the day you're going to win or lose. You never want a bill you are opposing to get out of committee and be debated on the floor."

James saw Kimberly walking across the floor with papers in her hands. She looked great, but he didn't mention her to Mike or Donald because she had told him she did not want attention drawn to her. She thought the less they knew about her personal life, the better off she and he were. James thought she was probably correct. James stood and told Donald and Mike he would be back in a few minutes, that he was going to walk the halls of the committee hearing rooms to see what was listed for the week. Leaving them at the table, he didn't tell Donald or Mike, but he was also going to catch up with Kimberly. She went into the bill room, and James waited down the hall for her to come out. When she came out, she saw him, and her smile went from ear to ear.

She walked over to James and said, "Good morning, Mr. James. I understand this is your first session of the legislature."

James, thinking for a second, responded, "Miss Kimberly, that's correct."

Then she leaned close to James and said, "Meet me in the basement by the broom closet door in three minutes."

She went one way, and he went the other. James met her, and they went into the broom closet and locked the door behind them. They started kissing in a wild passionate way.

"We better get out of here before we get found. If we get caught in here, we will be the news of the week among the bureaucrats and the lobbyists," Kimberly said.

"Goddamn, I would like to make love to you right now," James said.

"I would like for you to do that, but we have to get out of here now."

Then she reached down and felt his erection and said, "You need to get that down, boy."

She unzipped his pants and put her hand on his erection and teased him. Then like a fourth-grade schoolteacher ordering the children back into the classroom and off the playground, she said, "OK, boy, let's finish this later."

"Oh, no, now!" he said.

She insisted, and they left the broom closet. She said, "James, you should go that way. I'm going the other way."

James, with his pants protruding, walked back to the coffee shop. After a few minutes and out of hearing range of others, he called her and said, "Is this Kimberly's janitorial service?"

She laughed and said in a businesslike manner, "Yes, do you need something spruced up?"

"Yes, could I meet you in the broom closet immediately?"

"No, my services are closed for the day. Please call again after working hours for a full-service experience."

"You can depend on that for sure."

"I will talk to you later, James. Bye."

When James returned to the table, Donald said with a laugh, "Let's say you kill all the bills that you want to kill and pass the bills that your clients want to pass. Then you can go to the beach. Right? No, because any hour of any day the legislature is in session one of these assholes can offer an amendment that basically includes the entire bill you just defeated in committee. This means you have to sit here all fucking session and listen to every goddamn minute of every hour to make certain no amendment that negatively affects your clients is introduced. If you ever piss off one of those motherfuckers, they will introduce amendments just to fuck with you. The only good thing about this is that you will know more about the law than some lawyers after a few years, because you have heard it debated over and over again."

HANKY-PANKY

At breakfast James told Mike what he heard a group of lobbyists saying about sex and how it was not used to influence legislation. One said it was an unwritten rule. They all agreed that if a lobbyist tried to blackmail or threaten a legislator with extramarital sex exposure or any other form of sex, the entire group would ban that lobbyist. Members of the legislature would make certain the lobbyist never passed nor killed a bill. They would contact the lobbyist's clients and suggest another lobbyist. As a group they knew how to put a lobbyist out of business.

The lobbyist who was leading the conversation was known for securing women for the legislators. If a legislator wanted a woman, this lobbyist was the man to talk to. He was a sleazy kind of guy and was well known for this talent.

James asked Mike, "Do you think that sleazy lobbyist is an effective lobbyist?"

"I don't know. He has only one client, and the members of the group are sort of a sleazy bunch. Many legislators don't like his procurement activities."

"There is no place to hide an affair," one lobbyist had said at Donald's table the previous week. "Lobbyists know the legislators, and we are around the city day and night, and we talk to each other. When a legislator has an affair usually it is well known among us lobbyists."

"Oh, I forgot to tell you Donald's latest saying," James said. "The saying is, 'A little corruption is not so bad if you're getting your share. The only people complaining about corruption are those who are not getting their share.'"

"You never know what Donald is going to say next," Mike said, as he shook his head from side to side.

ONE BAD APPLE CAN SPOIL THE WHOLE BARREL

While walking to the capitol from the Greenhouse on a nice cool, sunshiny morning, Mike said that any bill the GOB wanted to pass needed two or more authors, according to a lobbyist he had met the day before.

James asked why, and Mike said the lobbyist told him that during his first session as a lobbyist he had a rich client who wanted a bill passed, so the client got a senator to introduce it. As the session rolled on, the bill did not come up for a hearing in committee. The lobbyist went to the senate while it was in session and called to the rail the senator who had authored the bill. He told the senator the session was going to end, and the bill had not been heard yet. The senator suggested they talk outside.

Outside in front of the capitol, the senator reminded the lobbyist that he was the only author listed on the bill, and if the author did not request the bill to be heard by committee, it would die without a hearing. Then the senator told him his bill was going to die unless his client gave him a one hundred thousand dollar campaign contribution.

"What happened after that?" James asked.

"I don't know, because the lobbyist left me standing as he ran after a house member he needed to talk to about a bill. But as he left, he turned and said, 'Don't get caught in that trap. Make sure you have multiple authors on all bills and a duplicate bill in the other chamber.'"

LITTLE RED RIDING HOOD AND THE WOLF

"The building materials dealers don't have a bill that would help or harm their businesses." James had noticed and pointed it out to Mike.

"With no wolf at the door, why hire us?" Mike asked.

"That's a good question, Mike."

At coffee the next morning, James asked Donald what to do if no legislation had been introduced that affected a client.

"Get a legislator to file a bill that will get their attention," Donald said. "Then the legislator doesn't bring up the bill for a hearing, and you tell your client you killed it. You will be the hero. If you don't want to deal with a bill, then ask a legislator to introduce an amendment, but you make no effort to kill it on the floor. Then in the next committee hearing, you get the amendment removed from the bill, and again you are the hero. They'll hire you again next year because you have proven that you can kill a bill or remove an amendment. What a great system it is for us lobbyists."

James, taken aback for a minute by Donald's remarks, said, "Donald, these methods are a little unethical, aren't they?"

"Yes, but it works every time, and it feels so good to be a hero."

James was shocked and didn't know how to react.

"You won't be the first lobbyists to screw over clients. Remember, a little unethical behavior is not so bad if it is helping your bottom line," Donald said with a laugh.

Their worry about no wolf at the door of the building materials dealers quickly came to a costly end one day. While sitting in the gallery of the house chamber one afternoon, Mike heard the word *lumber*. He realized that his building materials dealers could be involved. Some representative had added an amendment to tax lumber going into new buildings. It passed off the floor of the house of representatives without discussion.

He called James and said, "You're not going to believe this shit. The wolf just knocked on Red Riding Hood's door."

"What are you talking about?"

"We have a problem. If this renewal tax amendment that just sailed through the house is not killed, we're going to lose a client. We've got to kill it in the senate committee. Donald told me you can't fight something like this on the floor because it will consume all your time."

"Here we go again with these cards and letters," James said. "There has to be a better way. We need to call Phyllis and tell her we are on our way. Goddamn, Phyllis is expensive! Maybe we could hire someone to do some of this work and use Phyllis's service only when our employee can't do it."

Mike's mathematical mind started processing James's remark, and he said, "Maybe Nan, our university student worker, can do more of this work."

"That's a good idea, but we better stick with the real thing this round." They had a list of the material dealers and turned it over to Phyllis. She proceeded to take the same actions she had taken with the concrete people.

Again, like magic after the letters were sent, the phone calls started coming. The building materials dealers were calling, and they had connections. They had talked to the senators, and their responses were recorded on the war room wall. After one week of phone calls, it appeared Mike and James were two votes short of killing the amendment in the senate committee. It was time to talk to the man who told them to call him when they were in trouble, old Senator Jackson. That afternoon the boys headed to the Capitol House Bar, where the senator was, as usual, holding court in the booth with one of his paid-for girls.

CHAPTER 6

NEVER A DULL MOMENT

THE TREE HUGGERS

"Senator, we have a problem, but we don't know how to solve it," Mike said.

"What is it, boys?"

"A resource renewal tax of two percent has been added to House Bill 1635, and our building materials dealers don't like it."

"Well, you boys come up and play poker tonight, and we'll talk about it. I have room for both of you at the table at eight o'clock."

"Thank you, sir. We will be there," James said.

Upon arrival at the suite that evening for the card game, the senator, dressed in a house robe and house shoes with a cigar in his hand, told them, "Boys, I got a problem with this one. I read the amendment today after we talked. Them there environmentalists—you know, the tree-hugging motherfuckers—they have a bunch of bitches that track every bill that has the word *tree* in it. Then they stage a protest to get anyone who votes to kill a fucking tree defeated when he runs for reelection. Come step into the bedroom with me and let's talk."

Inside the bedroom Senator Jackson told them, "Boys, I'm willing to take on the tree huggers, but I will need some extra money for my reelection campaign. I'm especially concerned about having a connection to the killing of this resource renewal tax amendment because it will rally that guy from the Brown family in a town west of my home. That bastard gave me a bad time in the last election. He has so many family members in my district that he can almost get elected with just his family voting for him. Thank God most of them don't like one another. You know I'm on the Natural Resources Committee, and I can kill that thing for you boys. I almost guarantee it. But I need about five thousand dollars for my reelection campaign. Can you help me with that? You know I would do it for you boys whether you can raise the money or not, but it sure would be helpful and would make me a lot more enthusiastic. You know, and I do too, the damn tree huggers are going to come after me and anyone who I get to help me rip that damn amendment off the bill."

James immediately told the senator, "We will have five thousand for you by the end of the week. We thank you for helping us. We'll make certain that the building materials dealers in your district know you're the man who went to bat for them."

They lost the usual $500 each to the senator and didn't win it back.

That night leaving the hotel, Mike looked at James and said, "Where the fuck are you getting the five thousand dollars?"

"I guess we will be spending most of our expense money on things like this. We've got to keep the old man on our side, and we can't afford to lose the client. If he can swing the two votes, it's worth the money. Hell, we can't do it without him."

Mike suggested, "Let me talk to the president of the building materials dealers and ask them if they can raise a little money to help us out on this."

The next day Mike called the president and told him the situation. The next morning they had a check for $5,000 by express mail. A note inside said, "If you need any more help, let us know. Thanks for the good job. You boys are on your toes."

A week later the bill was posted on the senate's Natural Resources Committee wall. This meant it was going to be heard on Thursday of that week.

"We need to send out another notice reminding the building materials dealers to call their senators to remind them they need their help," James said. One of them had to testify before the committee.

Mike elected James. They developed a few talking points. James would tell the committee that the tax would increase the cost of construction, that the building materials companies already encouraged timber companies to replant, and that it was just an unnecessary tax.

To their surprise the construction lobbyists joined in and testified to kill the tax. Mike and James didn't realize construction lobbyists were going to be there to testify.

"Damn, we may not have had to spend the five thousand," James said.

A motion was made to remove the renewal resource tax amendment that had been placed on the bill during the debate in the house of representatives. James and Mike and the building materials dealers won by only one vote, which was cast by the chairperson of the committee.

Now the bill was headed to the senate floor, and hopefully the tree huggers couldn't get someone to reattach the amendment. The next week when the bill came up for debate on the senate floor, the Good Ole Boys listened intently. The amendment was never discussed, and the tree huggers were absent. There was still one risk. Now the bill would go to Conference Committee, and the governor would appoint three from the senate and three from the house to merge the senate version and the house version.

James ran into Paul the lobbyist and asked him how the Conference Committee worked. Paul told him not to worry about that; the senate always won. That is, almost always. Plus, nothing could be done about it now but to cross one's fingers.

"You might have one of your building materials dealers contact the governor, but that would draw attention to it, and it might go the other way," Paul said. "Go fishing and forget about it."

Paul was correct. The final bill signed by the governor did not mention a renewable resource tax on lumber. GOB and Associates Incorporated had scored its first victory for the building materials dealers.

At one of the legislative parties, Mike and James were talking to Mary Ann, the lead lobbyist for the Association of Contractors, about how they could work together.

Mary Ann said, "The building materials dealers' renewable tax amendment was an issue that both your group and mine were certainly interested in. The tax would have driven up the cost of construction and made buildings harder to sell, not to mention all the extra paperwork for collecting and paying the tax. We should have been counting votes together." She listed the senators who agreed to vote with them, and one of them was Senator Jackson. Then to James and Mike's surprise, Mary Ann told them Jackson was the first to agree to help them. He had called them the first day the amendment was introduced and told the contractors he would kill it for them.

Then Mary Ann said calmly, "We give him a lot of money every election year, and he is always with us."

A light went on in Mike and James's head. Mary Ann moved on to talk to someone else.

"It had been almost two weeks after the amendment was introduced when we met with the senator. We have been taken for five thousand dollars by our best barroom and poker-playing friend, Senator Jackson. He was planning to kill the amendment for the contractors all the time. He had no fear of the tree huggers as he stated," James said.

Mike expressed his anger. "That goddamn son of a bitch fucked us!"

"We have a lot to learn," James said. "Some of these lessons are very expensive. Can you believe that old bastard? I thought he was our best buddy."

"We live and learn, don't we!"

"It's all about money. There seems to be honor among thieves. He did vote for us." They both laughed and moved on to socialize with others.

That night Kimberly invited James to dinner at her condo. The dining-room table was already set when he arrived. She planned to treat him like a warrior returning home after winning a great battle. James went to one end of the table. Kimberly pulled out the chair for him and told him to be seated. He laughed but followed her instructions. His favorite wine was on the table waiting for him in a nice stemmed glass adorned with a beautifully etched design.

Kimberly went to the adjoining kitchen and returned with the first of a five-course meal she had prepared for him.

"Can I help?" he asked.

"No, you are the victor—the warrior returning home, and to the victor go the spoils. I had to postpone the ticker-tape parade because of the rain. You won a serious legislative battle today. I'm so proud of you."

Kimberly and James had not been together since the broom closet, so he had a lot to tell her.

While they ate, she listened intently, rarely commenting other than to say, "That's wonderful, you guys are great" and other complimentary words.

After his second glass of wine, James whispered, "We have talked enough about business for the night, Miss Kimberly. You left a job unfinished in the broom closet."

She smiled and said, "I will try to complete the job before the night is over."

A big smile came to his face. "Completion of the job would be appreciated."

After dessert they cleaned the dishes and put them away. Kimberly said, "Oh, James, I have a gift for you."

"What, another one?"

James acted like he was complaining, but he really enjoyed her gifts.

"Yes, another one, and I don't want any backtalk. Open it."

James opened the package with his careful unwrapping technique. It was a box from a nice men's store with a beautiful silk tie in it. "Kimberly, I have never been treated so nice by anyone in my entire life. You are going to go broke if you keep spending all this money on me."

Kimberly, ignoring his comment, said, "I plan to make you very happy, and when I'm finished, you might be the best-dressed lobbyist in the state capitol."

By morning Kimberly had finished the broom closet job and more. James had spent the night with her for the first time. James, being an early riser, was up and made coffee for Kimberly. He brought in the newspaper that was delivered to her door and read most of it before she came out.

When he saw her, James said, "You are beautiful in the morning."

"Thanks. Comments like that will get you anything you want. What's in the paper that's interesting?"

"I suppose the most interesting thing is that the state has three US congressmen who are leaving office in the next six years. We will have some new blood, I suppose. None of them are interested in improving the state. They are all voting as instructed by some special interest group, hoping to get a lucrative lobbying job while drawing a retirement check from Congress. Did you know the last one got a two million dollar signing bonus to sign on as a lobbyist for Z Company?"

"That's interesting. You should run for Congress, James."

"Oh no. I'm developing a lobbying firm. In addition, Kimberly, if I won, I would be in Washington, DC, and you would be here in the capital city."

"No, I would be in Washington with you."

A GIFT—HOW DARE YOU!

At the office the next day James and Mike talked about what was said at the coffee shop and other places that week. While James cooked breakfast, Mike told him what Bobby the lobbyist had told the coffee group the day before. Bobby said a guy on the legislative staff told him that during Christmas he received so many steaks and hams he had to buy a freezer to keep them. A statewide elected official would likely not remember which lobbyist gave her a ham, but a state worker appreciated it. Bobby said most state workers would take a ham or a few steaks, but they would never do anything dishonest. Most lobbyists at the table agreed that the large majority of state employees were wonderful workers and would never take part in dishonest activities. The group also agreed that in a large population, there were a few bureaucrats who were just absolutely crooks.

As an example, Bobby said he took a bottle of whiskey to a state worker during the Christmas holidays. The state worker handed it back to him and abruptly said he couldn't take it, that it would be dishonest. One year later this SOB was indicted by a federal grand jury for soliciting a $50,000 bribe from a contractor. In other words, this state employee was a real phony who took large bribes but refused the bottle of whiskey.

"I'm encouraged; there are a lot of people with integrity around here," Mike said. "We learn more every day, don't we?" James nodded his head yes.

OIL AND WATER DO NOT MIX

The theater bill was coming up for hearing in about three weeks. Mike and James decided to invite all the theater managers to the capital city for a grassroots day. This was their first big mistake. The theater managers were not the kind of people who were going to convince legislators to vote their way. They were the artistic type. These strange, different, and unique individuals spoke when they should've been listening.

To top off the disaster, the motorcycle helmet law was being heard that day. Combining the theater managers and the motorcycle riders was like mixing oil and water. At one point one of the managers screamed in the hallway because one of the motorcycle riders pinched him on the ass. Due to a bomb threat, the capitol was evacuated that afternoon. The building search by the bomb squad took so much time that it resulted in the cancellation of the committee hearings for the day. The theater manager bill was moved to the next week, and the motorcycle helmet law hearing was moved to the week after that.

That evening after things had calmed down, James said, "Thank God for the cancellation. It just wasn't working out with those two groups in the same building. We do not need the theater managers at grassroots day next week. Maybe some rich people who are interested in theater, but the theater managers themselves may be a handicap rather than a benefit."

James strategized aloud. "We should get on the phone with the donor list provided by the theater managers and encourage them to call the legislators to see if that can sway a few votes."

"Yes," said Mike, "but we should only call those who have donated more than twenty thousand dollars."

The next morning they started calling. From some they got answers such as, "No, I'm not calling those scumbags."

There were several positive responses. After three days they had a tie vote on the senate committee because most of the donors were rich people who had political connections.

On the day of the hearing, James invited three theater managers to testify. The vote came down to a tie, and the chairman of the committee broke the tie, killing the bill. The theater managers were disappointed, but one said, "We did much better than I thought we would."

"We now have a year to work on next year's legislation. We should focus on who knows whom," James suggested.

Then he told the managers, "I really believe in what you're trying to do. You can bring theater arts to a new level in the history of our state. Maybe we should think of some alternative ways, such as a tax credit or a special deduction for donors."

"We have a year to think about it, but we must realize that if it's this difficult to get out of the committee, it's also going to be very difficult on the floor," Mike said. "Passing the bill is going to take much more time than we anticipated. In next year's legislation, we need to include a statewide board to oversee theater funding so we can put some of the legislators and their families on those boards and pay them for attending. The funds could come from the taxes they would pass.

We can put one of us on the board to help us recoup from our low fees we're charging your group."

The theater managers all agreed. Mike added, "We will have to revise our contract during the year."

One of the theater managers said, "No problem," and they all nodded their heads in agreement.

After the theater managers departed, Mike said to James, "This is not a bad deal for us. We would be guaranteed an annual income just for sitting on a board we created."

They both laughed, and James said, "Maybe we should create more boards. They could become a major profit center for us."

"You are damn right!" Mike replied.

HELMETS AND HOGS

The next week a helmet bill was heard at the legislature. James and Mike were just observers. They had been told by other lobbyists to get a seat in the committee room because it was going to be an interesting day.

The helmet bill was one of the most politically fascinating hearings of the session. The bill would require individuals riding motorcycles to wear a helmet. This bill truly divided the right and left wings of political philosophy. Among Mike and James's friends outside the legislative arena, this was the most discussed bill in the legislature. It made people think about politics. Persons who had no intention of ever riding a motorcycle became interested in this bill because it exemplified what some thought was government intervention into personal lives. It brought politics to the simplest level. Everyone could understand it.

Each year a representative from the southern part of the state introduced the bill. This brought out a large group of strange bed partners. People who would not acknowledge one another on the street were all of a sudden on the same side. Men in three-piece suits and ties were walking the hallways of the capitol with people who had tattoos from their neck to their feet and a few with tattoos on their faces.

This was the bill the conservatives saw as a chance to bring attention to what they thought was too much government involvement in the personal life of individuals. They advocated that a person had a right to ride in the open air without having to wear a hood over his head. They proclaimed it was like the legislature was trying to kill Easy Rider.

The motorcycle hogs rolled around the capitol like Indians surrounding a wagon train, waving their hands, revving their engines, and screaming at the top of their lungs, "Kill the goddamn bill, kill the goddamn bill." At other times the hog riders walked the capitol, saying, "Who in the hell gave these sons of bitches the right to tell us what to wear? What happened to freedom?" They claimed they had a right to die if they wanted.

There were so many motorcycle riders in the hallways of the capitol that it was difficult for lobbyists and legislators to carry on regular business. James and Mike couldn't walk through the capitol hallway without bumping into one of them, and they certainly didn't want to piss off any of them. They wore multiple chains around their necks, earrings and nose rings, long hair and beards, black boots, and leather jackets with club names like Hell's Angels. Some of the women looked like they could whip any man in the building. It was a spectacular event. It turned a normally dignified state legislature into a zoo of weirdos.

As always, there was another side to the story. The other view was the fact that injuries caused by motorcycle wrecks were costing the citizens of the state a great deal of money. When motorcyclists were injured, many did not have insurance and were admitted to a hospital's emergency room, where the state had to pick up the tab.

The author of the bill came up with a creative way to illustrate the problem. He waited outside the committee hearing room with a round watermelon and a baseball bat. When his turn to testify came, he walked in and aggressively continued to the table where he was to testify. He placed the watermelon on the table. He immediately swung the baseball bat at the watermelon, hitting it and splattering it all over the room, including on the clothes of representatives on the committee.

The chairman of the committee screamed to the sergeant at arms, "Grab that man and take that damn bat away from him! Is he crazy? Look what he did to my suit and tie!"

"Are you a damn idiot?" one member of the committee hollered.

"You're going to get a big laundry bill!" another said.

"I just wanted you gentlemen to see what somebody's head looks like after a motorcycle accident without a helmet. I heard about a state representative from another state doing the same thing, but maybe it wasn't a good idea, judging by how upset some of you committee members are," the author said defensively.

"Gentlemen, the taxpayers have to pay to try to put the motorcyclists' heads back together. I'm tired of taking care of these irresponsible motorcycle riders who don't have health insurance. They are costing the state millions of dollars just to buy wheelchairs."

The room was out of control, and the sergeant at arms was seeking backup. Three more security guards entered the room. The motorcycle dudes were screaming at the top of their voices, "Throw him out! Throw him out! Throw the bastard out!" The chairman was threatening to have all the motorcycle riders arrested. The news reporters were scrambling to report the story. The television cameras were rolling inside and outside the committee room. When the representatives left the committee room, every TV station in the state wanted to interview the author of the bill and the chairman of the committee. They surrounded the melon buster like hummingbirds around a freshly filled bird feeder.

One legislator had a suggestion that seemed to solve the problem by requiring $30,000 in insurance for anyone who rode a motorcycle without a helmet. Under this bill, a person would be allowed to ride a motorcycle without a helmet as long as he had proof he had insurance coverage. The bikers didn't like it nor did those who demanded higher insurance limits. They claimed that treatment for most injuries cost much more than thirty thousand. Some, however, loved it, including the insurance companies, because after the bill passed, they sold more insurance. The hospitals and doctors received some money, whereas in the past, most motorcycle injuries were charity cases.

"One way or another, and I'm not certain how, the lawyers will enjoy some benefits," Mike said.

"I suppose the lawyers sue the insurance companies," James responded.

Who was right and who was wrong, the Good Ole Boys didn't know. Mike and James could argue both sides for certain. They agreed that the compromise was a good answer. There is an old saying, "When both sides are unhappy, it generally is a good compromise."

"I'm just glad we were not involved in the lobbying process related to this bill," Mike said.

After the bill passed and was signed into law by the governor, there were the diehards. They wore skullcaps that looked like a Jewish yarmulke. For a while they skirted around the law with these small yarmulkes that barely met the standards set forth in the law.

James and Mike thought that hearing would be one of the most controversial they would ever see. However, they didn't know what was coming the next session when they represented the mental health workers.

FEEDING THE MONKEYS

James casually walked into Mike's office, took a seat, and said, "Mike, I want to tell you what I saw today. I couldn't believe my eyes. I'm sure you remember the lobbyist for the ABC Fortune 500 company who has the personality of a brick wall and never says anything at Donald's table. You know him. His name is Larry. He's a big guy. We have seen him in the coffee shop several times, and he gets his shoes shined every morning. You may remember that Donald told us he was one of the most influential people in the state capitol.

"Well, he uses a lobbying technique that I'm going to refer to as 'feeding the monkeys.' I'm going to name it that because it's just like training monkeys. If a monkey does something that you approve of, and you give the monkey a banana, then the monkey is likely to do it again and again and again as long as you're feeding him bananas. I saw him hand a legislator a white envelope and wondered what was in it. I asked Paul about it.

"Paul said Larry has staff in the company's public relations department who follow all the bills in the state legislature and look for anything that might affect the company he represents. Each morning before the legislature convenes, his staff prints a check for each committee member who would vote yes or no on a bill or bills that his company is interested in passing or killing. Larry the lobbyist then travels to the state capitol with the checks in his right-side suit pocket.

"Paul laughed about it. He said the checks are dimensionally large enough to be slightly seen in Larry's pocket. Larry then searches and finds each committee member and approaches him with the following question: 'Senator, my company is interested in senate or house bill number so-and-so. Can you vote for us on that bill?' He would explain the bill to the legislator, if needed. All the time Larry is making his spiel, he is shuffling or thumbing the checks in his suit pocket like a card dealer would thumb a deck of playing cards. The thumbing of the checks makes a shuffling noise. If the senator or representative says he will support and vote the way Larry wants him to vote, he will then take a check out of his pocket and give it to the legislator.

"If the legislator says he cannot vote the way the Fortune 500 company wants him to vote, then Larry will politely say, 'Thank you for talking with me. Our company always appreciates your consideration of legislation we are interested in,' and walks away. No check given. The monkey does not get the banana. Can you believe it?

"This routine goes on day after day. The monkeys, meaning the legislators, learned quickly that a positive response got a banana or a check, which just so happened to be just under the Campaign Financial Disclosure Act requirements. There is no record of the contribution, and nothing illegal was done. Paul said that's why the Fortune 500 companies are so interested and involved in writing the campaign contribution limits and rules. The monkeys always look forward to seeing Larry when they are voting for his company's legislative interest."

"The question becomes, is this good government or not?" James asked.

Mike leaned back in his chair. "It depends on whether you work for the Fortune 500 company or not. It certainly is good government from the company's point of view."

"It's hard to lose in a monkey cage when you have a pocket full of bananas." They both laughed and moved onto another subject.

James called Kimberly. He told her about feeding the monkeys.

"Welcome to the real world of American politics," she said. "Remember the golden rule. Those who have the gold make the rules."

James had no idea how well Kimberly understood the phrase "feeding the monkeys." Her family had fed many monkeys.

CHAPTER 7

BROWN IS THE GOB'S BEST COLOR

THIS PLACE IS CRAZY; I'M QUITTING

As James cooked bacon and eggs for breakfast one morning at the Greenhouse, Mike said, "I have been wondering where you got certain information, such as the library tax, the three sessions to pass it, and the concrete lobbyist retiring." Then, before James could answer, he continued, "You seem to always bring these little rabbits out of the hat just at the right time. Are you getting this information from other lobbyists?"

"No, not from other lobbyists, but from a nice lady at the capitol," he said, but he didn't tell Mike Kimberly's name. "She's been helping me with information I need. She's a valuable source of information."

"Damn, we need to hire her," Mike said.

"I don't think so. It appears she doesn't need us. I think she's happy where she is."

"Are you screwing her?"

James had learned as a young boy not to kiss and tell. He replied almost instantly, "She is a nice lady who tries to help everyone."

"Be good to her. We damn sure need her."

ELDERLY TIMBER LOBBYIST QUITS

"I talked to an elderly timber lobbyist today, and I cannot get over what he told me," Mike said. "He said he was quitting his job representing timber because it was getting to where he couldn't work with legislators anymore. I asked him why not? He said, 'The goddamn feds will try to put lobbyists and legislators in jail for a little simple thing like handing out a few dollars to our legislative friends to help them in their reelection campaigns. If they keep this up, only the rich will be able to serve. I went to my company's accountant this morning to get the forty thousand dollar check that I always took to the bank and cashed every session so I could provide a little cash to my legislator friends—at least those who voted the way I needed them to. The damn accountant told me the rules had changed and sent me to the company lawyer, who told me I couldn't hand out the money anymore because it was illegal. I told him I had done it for years, so why stop now? The lawyer told me it was because FBI agents would arrest me and put my butt in jail. I asked him who in the fuck was going to tell the feds, and he told me they were wiretapping everyone down there at the state capitol. I told him, that goddamn lawyer, how the hell am I going to get anything done down here without money. All the legislative leaders expect me to be at the front door of the capitol at a set time to hand out the money. I'm going to have to tell them I don't have any. You think they're going to be my friends anymore? Hell no! This place is all about cash. You never have any real friends here. When the money's gone, you're gone. So I quit. I'm just here today to thank all my old buddies for all the years of help. I'm going to enjoy retirement, and I wish all you boys good luck.'"

"Did you ask him if the timber company has hired any-one to replace him?"

"Yes, I did, and he gave me the name of the person to call about representing the Brown Timber Company. He said they own more than one million acres of land and have mills in seven different states, but their headquarters are in our state. I've already called him and have an appointment tomorrow, just after the legislature returns. He's coming to have lunch with us at the Greenhouse."

"Damn, Mike, that's great!"

The next day at a quarter to one, the owner of Brown Timber Company, Mr. Dwight, walked in the door of the Greenhouse. He was a short but athletic looking man in his late fifties. He had overgrown eyebrows, but his eyes were a beautiful shade of blue. Several legislators had already eaten lunch. The place was full except for one seat. James, who had an amazing memory for names, walked Mr. Dwight around the room and introduced him to each of the senators and representatives. James told them where he was from and that he was the owner of Brown Timber Company.

Mr. Dwight enjoyed talking to the senators and represen-tatives. After the room cleared, James and Mike invited Mr. Dwight into James's office to talk business while the cook cleaned. The three men sat around the desk and talked about the different senators and representatives. Mr. Dwight told them he was highly impressed by their operation.

He asked if all lobbyists had such a place as a Greenhouse.

"No, we are the only ones," James responded.

"This is a genius idea, and the GOB are obviously going to be super lobbyists." Then he said, "I'm going to take a chance on the GOB." He laughed. "That is what you're calling yourselves, right?"

James and Mike laughed and said, "Yes!"

"Brown Timber will pay you one hundred thousand dollars per year and give you forty-five thousand dollars for fundraising invitations and other expenses. You will not have to account for your expenses to Brown Timber; that accounting will be between you and the IRS. Brown does not want to be involved in any problems you might have with the IRS, so the forty-five thousand will be shown as a part of your fee. Ninety thousand dollars will be wired immediately to your account, and the remainder of your fee will be wired at the end of the legislative session. You will receive all the money whether you win or lose. If you lose, Brown Timber is not going to like it. If you win, that would be great. I'll write you a letter confirming this contract, and I will have our accounting office wire ninety thousand dollars to your account. I will need your routing number and checking account number. We will also need a tax identification number. You should be forewarned that Brown reports all contractors' wages and fees to the IRS. You will receive a 1099 from Brown. At Brown Timber we believe that everyone should pay his taxes. OK, boys, do we have a deal?"

Mike and James simultaneously agreed.

"Also, I forgot to point out, Brown has three private airplanes, and any one of them is available to you at anytime for entertaining or business travel. When the three of us need to meet, I will send a plane to pick you up. There's one other thing you need to know about Brown. We're very interested in oil and gas legislation because one-third of our properties have oil or gas deposits on them, and we have to keep an eye on the big oil companies. They can't be trusted.

"Now, before I leave, and that must be immediately, I have some information for you that should make you happy. I called the governor before I came, and he said he was very impressed with you guys. He said you had some heavy-duty connections. He told me he had heard of the Greenhouse and he thought you had the enthusiasm, the smartness, and the ability to act, as well as being excellent persuaders. As you know, bullshitting counts in your business."

They all laughed and Mr. Dwight departed.

Just after the limo was out of sight, Mike said calmly to James, "Can you believe that? Interviewed, checked out, and hired overnight."

"I'll bet he did a background check on us!"

"Do you think so?"

"Yes," James said.

"Then we must have checked out."

"No, it wasn't a background check; it was the governor. He's the one who got us hired," James said.

"Hell, the governor doesn't know us. He wouldn't recognize us if he saw us on the street," Mike said.

"You're right. I wonder why he recommended us, and who told him about the Greenhouse?"

"The governor said we had some heavy-duty connections? What in the hell is he talking about? Certainly he's not talking about old Senator Jackson," Mike said.

"Maybe he got us confused with someone else. What the hell! We'll take a good recommendation from him any day," James said.

What the good ole boys didn't know was that the magic wand was working again. The heavy-duty connections the governor was talking about was Kimberly's father, a man they had never met.

TIMBER CLIENTS CELEBRATION DINNER

When the Greenhouse cleared, James and Mike each opened a beer and propped their feet up on the table.

"What a great day!" James cried out.

"I'm going to take my wife out for a big celebration dinner tonight," Mike said.

"I would like to come and bring a friend of mine," James said.

"OK, that's great."

"Good."

"We will see you at Joey's restaurant at eight o'clock tonight. What's your friend's name?"

"Kimberly."

Just after that conversation, Kimberly called. James told her about the new client. "Great, I'm dating a winner."

"That's correct, we are kicking ass. Mike and his wife have invited us to go to dinner with them tonight. Would you like to go?"

"Of course I want to go. I wouldn't miss this celebration for anything."

"May I pick you up at seven?"

"No, I'm working late. I will meet you at your apartment at seven thirty."

"That will work. I'll see you at seven thirty."

Kimberly arrived at James's apartment as planned and had a gift for him. As usual, he complained but opened it.

"This is a gift in celebration of a major victory," Kimberly said.

James opened the gift and found a watch—a Cartier watch.

He put it on and said, "It really looks great. I love it!" James did not know much about watches and did not realize it was a very expensive watch.

The two couples drove into the parking lot of Joey's restaurant at the same time. They walked to the door, and as usual Joey's was busy. A table would be ready in thirty minutes.

Mike asked his usual question, "Where did you two meet?"

"Kimberly is on the legislative staff," James said. "We met in the broom closet."

"We did not meet in the broom closet. Behave yourself, James."

"What do you do on the legislative staff?" Mike asked.

"I am a bill drafter and researcher."

"I wondered why James was always ready to go to the capitol," Mike said. "How long have you known each other?"

"About three months before the session started," Kimberly said.

"James, you never mentioned Kimberly," Mike said.

"Because she wants to have a low profile. She thinks you should keep your personal relationships out of the capitol, and we have."

"You're right about that," Mike said. "You have certainly kept your relationship a secret from me and everyone else in the capitol, and that's hard to do." They all laughed.

Mike's wife noticed James's watch because she also had a Cartier watch. "James, I've never noticed your watch before. Have you had it long?"

"No, Kimberly gave it to me today."

"Very, very nice," Mike's wife said.

James noticed her reaction and thought maybe the watch was more expensive than he realized, or maybe it was just a knock-off of some stylish brand.

They each had a martini while waiting for a table. Mike ordered a bottle of Dom Pérignon champagne and very expensive wine during dinner. They stayed in the restaurant until eleven talking about this and that. The check was outrageous, but they didn't care. They knew they were celebrating the beginning of a major lobbying organization.

Mike's wife quizzed Kimberly several times about her personal life but never learned any more than she was a state employee on the legislative staff. In the back of her mind, she was wondering how a state employee could afford a Cartier watch.

On their way home, Mike's wife told him, "That Cartier watch Kimberly gave James is real. I know it when I see a knock-off, and there are very few Cartier knock-offs. Cartier strictly enforces its copyrights worldwide."

"I don't think James knows what a Cartier watch is. If he does, he probably thinks the watch is a knock-off. Plus, if she wants to spend her money, she couldn't find a better man than James to spend it on," Mike said.

REPORTERS, THE SOBS

It was a beautiful spring day and Mike was sitting outside on the capitol steps. A reporter sat beside him and asked if he could talk to him about what happened with the theater bill.

"Sure."

"Of course your remarks will be off the record," the reporter said.

"What do you want to know?" Mike asked.

Basically the reporter wanted to know what was going on behind the scenes related to the theater tax bill. Mike explained to him where the bill was and who was paying for the lobbyists and so on. He explained that the bill was not a tax increase. It just redistributed the property taxes that were being collected. The reporter continued to take notes as Mike talked. "This is off the record, isn't it?" Mike asked.

The young reporter assured Mike that his name would not be used. The next morning on the front page of the capital city newspaper was almost everything Mike had said, plus much he had not said, and his name was used several times. Some statements had been just made up by the reporter. The headline for the article read, "Theaters Failed to Increase Property Tax—Will Try Again."

The article created a backlash among the antitax crowd. The GOB office received threatening phone calls. The caller would not listen when the GOB told them it was not a tax increase and the bill was dead. "The callers are so extreme,"

James said. "Do you think we need to buy a gun to protect ourselves?"

"Hell, no, I'm not carrying a goddamn pistol," Mike replied.

"I hope one of the crazy bastards doesn't kill us," James said. "The phone calls have been unbelievable, and I think we should turn some of the written threats over to the FBI. The callers want schools, roads, and defense, but they don't want to pay taxes for them, much less pay a tax for little theaters."

Fortunately, the article was about the theater managers Mike and James represented, and they were just happy to be in the paper. "Any recognition is better than none at all," said one theater manager.

"Thank goodness it was not concrete, timber, or some client like that. They would've fired us instantly," James said. "We should never trust a newspaper reporter again. The young ones have less ethics than some lobbyists. They will print to further their careers."

"OK. From this day forward we will issue news releases," Mike said, "but we will never talk to reporters again."

"I agree; they are a bunch of son of a bitches and they could get one of us killed."

WHY BROWN TIMBER NEEDS THE GOB

At their breakfast meeting a few days later, the question arose as to why Brown Timber might need a lobbyist.

"Other than monitoring what is happening and making certain there are no more surprises like the tax amendment that almost nailed the building materials dealers, I'm not certain why Brown Timber Company needs us," Mike said. "There's no legislation that has an impact on them that I know about." Neither Mike nor James was certain of the answer.

Later during a telephone conversation, James told Kimberly about Mike's question. "Oh, yes, there is a reason Brown needs you," she said. "There's a right-of-way bill related to fencing all properties that could cost Brown millions of dollars. I will research the number for you."

"Please do. We don't want to lose that private airplane service. Without it we may never be able to join the mile-high club."

"Men are always thinking about is sex," Kimberly said.

"Wouldn't you like to join the mile-high club with me?"

"Maybe. It would depend on how private the cabin is."

"We will have to continue this conversation another day. It sounds exciting. As a matter of fact, I have a vision of the mile-high club in my mind right now," James said.

"Down, boy, we need to get back to business." Kimberly looked up the bill concerning the right-of-way and called James back to give him the number.

"I don't know how we missed this one," James said in a low voice.

"There are so many bills that it's easy to miss something like this. Plus, many times such items are hidden in a little paragraph at the bottom of the bill because the author doesn't want anyone to notice them. Items like this one often slide through without anyone noticing until it becomes law."

James got a copy of the bill and called Mr. Dwight with Brown Timber Company.

Their conversation went like this: James told him good afternoon, followed by some small talk about the nice weather and a short discussion about a national political issue.

Then James got down to business. "I called to tell you about a right-of-way bill that you may have an interest in." James then read a summary of the bill to him.

"Don't worry about the bill. I'll take care of it," Mr. Dwight said. "What is the number of the bill?"

"How will you take care of it?"

"For your information only, Senator Jones and Representative Roy are in our pocket. If anything else comes up that is adverse to Brown, just call them, and they will take care of it for us. They can't afford not to. We could put somebody in the race just to make their lives miserable. Just the votes of our employees and their families could defeat them."

"That's good to know."

"Thanks for keeping your eye out for us. You and Mike are doing a great job."

"Thank you."

Like clockwork a few days later, Representative Roy and Senator Jones hustled the votes to have the fencing wording stripped from the bill in committee.

Mike suggested to James, "When we're not busy in the office, I think we should spend more of our time at the state capitol. One of us always needs to be there to be certain none of those SOB's introduce another amendment like they did with the building materials dealers. Those old lobbyists teach us a lot."

"That's true, and they have some great stories," James said. "We are only a few days into the session, and as far as we know, we don't have a bill coming up in the next couple of weeks. Let's spend that time in the coffee shop social-izing and learning more about this business. But we need to be here in the Greenhouse for lunch to greet the legislators. We can talk to the lobbyists at the capitol. I don't think we should invite other lobbyists to the Greenhouse. Why pay for their entertainment?"

"I agree," Mike said. "Nan, our wonderful student worker who can do anything on a computer, can order the food. The cook prepares the lunches, so we don't need to be there."

"Did you know Nan has been ordering the food from a store on the phone? It's delivered to the Greenhouse free!"

"No, you can do that?"

"Yes," James said. "We've been so busy, I thought the cook was buying the food at a grocery store."

CHAPTER 8

TRUSTED ADVICE

HOW HIGH IS THAT HILL

At one of their breakfast meetings, Mike told James about a lobbyist who was trying to convince the legislature to pass a bill that would allow his company to dump a pile of hazardous waste material in the river. The material in large quantities was radioactive. He wanted an exception from the state's environmental rules by means of legislation. Mike was sitting on the couch outside the senate, and next to him was the lobbyist who was sponsoring the hazardous waste radioactive bill.

The lobbyist said to Mike, "I know you have been sitting here listening to them arguing my bill. I would like to ask you some questions about the bill."

"Sure, fire away!"

"How high do you think the pile of hazardous waste is?" Mike noticed he said *pile*, not *hill* or *mountain*.)

"Probably thirty or forty feet high."

The lobbyist, with a smile on his face, said, "Perfect!"

By his response Mike could tell that the hill was taller than he thought. "How tall is that damn hill?"

"Taller than a thirty-story building," the lobbyist replied.

Knowing the pile was that high, Mike could only imagine how wide it was.

"If you think it's only thirty or forty feet high, then so do the members of the senate because you have heard the same arguments they have," the lobbyist said. "That's great news because I'm going to pass this bill and be able to dump that mountain of waste in that small river. Of course, some of the people who use the water downstream will be radioactive for a few days, but so what. They need to be a little brighter anyway. Thanks for answering my question. You have been a big help."

He passed the bill out of the senate and through the house, and the governor signed it. The waste was dumped into the river.

The company saved millions by using this shortcut to hazardous waste disposal. To celebrate, the lobbyist bought everyone at the Capitol House Bar a round of drinks.

"I'm certain those downriver citizens glowed in the dark for a few days," Mike said to James. "There was never any newspaper or television coverage or any public outcry."

"Whether you like what this man did or not, he was a good lobbyist," James said. "What a great system for those of us in it. He represented his client and achieved what the client paid him to do. I'm happy we never had a client that involved us in such a bill. Would we have done what this man did? It would be easy to say no, we would not, but it's interesting how money influences decisions."

"We're no different from anyone else," Mike said. "At what point will we not be able to sleep at night?"

Kimberly called James and said, "We need to go by the apartment to see what you need to make it more livable and comfortable."

"It's already furnished. What else could it need?"

"I don't know, but maybe a few things. See you there at five." At five James drove into the driveway, and Kimberly was already there in the apartment.

On the table was a large package wrapped in gift paper. Kimberly said, "I got you something for the apartment."

"That's a big box. What could it be?"

"Well, open it, silly, and see what it is." James carefully unwrapped the box and removed the item. It was a Disney character telephone.

"You have Mickey Mouse in the office, so you need Goofy for the apartment," Kimberly said.

"This is great! I love it. Thank you so much. You're always thinking of me. I've never bought you anything. You are so wonderful, sexy, intelligent, and the best friend I've had in years."

"Damn, keep talking, and I may have to get Minnie Mouse for you as well."

James put the phone on the table, walked over to Kimberly, and kissed her passionately. It didn't take long for the kiss to turn into lovemaking.

Afterward, with a serious face, James said, "We need to talk seriously about our relationship, what it's all about and what we expect of each other."

"James, I don't expect anything of you other than for you to marry me and for us to have children."

"Whoa, this is a little fast, isn't it? We can't fall in love. I'm just now separated from my wife. I would prefer to call this recreational sex."

"Recreational sex is OK as long as you marry me."

"Let's talk about this later."

"Oh, I'm making you a little nervous, I see." She laughed and tickled him in the ribs until he laughed.

James's apartment phone rang. It was Mike calling. He was at the Capitol House Bar and asked James if he was coming by the bar.

James told him yes. Then he looked at Kimberly and said, "I have to go do a little business. I will talk to you tomorrow."

"Have fun with the boys. I'll miss you."

A GETAWAY FROM THE GAME

After dealing with all the phone calls and the problems associated with the job, James needed a break. He asked Kimberly if she would like to go sailing with him. She enthusiastically replied, "Yes, Captain James!"

James laughed and said, "We will leave from your condo at five. I will pick you up after I buy the wine."

"I will bring nibbles."

What James did not know was that Kimberly had sailed on several serious yachts. She had sailed in the Indian Ocean, Mediterranean Sea, the Atlantic, and the South Pacific, but she wasn't telling James. James was proud of his little sailboat, and she did not want to make him think she didn't appreciate it. Nor did she want to bring up anything in the conversation that might reveal her wealth. She wanted to know for certain that James cared for her, and not for her wealth.

James had bought a small sailboat a few years before he met Kimberly. The hull of the boat was white, and the sail covers were blue. Made by Flickr, the boat was twenty feet long, weighed nearly six thousand pounds, and had a three-foot keel. The deck trim and interior of the cabin were made of teak, and it had headroom for a person six feet tall or more. It was certainly the "Mercedes" of small sailboats. It was moored in an inland lake north of the city.

James spent more time maintaining the boat than he did sailing. He enjoyed doing the maintenance work, though. It took his mind off the daily stresses of life. He took friends out for sunset cocktails, and occasionally he would anchor overnight off a small island in the middle of the lake. He participated in local regattas with friends but was not a competitive racer. He had a bowling trophy that had been given to him by a crew member after a regatta in which he had finished last. He kept it on board and occasionally showed it to people and told them that in the last regatta, the yacht club ran out of trophies and gave him the old bowling trophy. He was amazed at how many people believed him. After having a minute to think about what James had said, everyone would laugh.

During the cocktail hour, James wore a T-shirt with an image of a tuxedo on the front and back. He put it on to serve the wine to Kimberly. She laughed and enjoyed his humor. Sailing with James was fun. There was none of that testosterone-driven spirit that she had experienced among the overly competitive sailors she had known. It was relaxing and enjoyable.

Many times James would spend the weekend working on the sailboat or just enjoying the lake environment. In his former business careers, the boat was not much of an advantage, but as a lobbyist, it could be an asset. As soon as the politicians and lobbyists learned of James's boat, they would invite themselves, and James would take them on a sunset cocktail sail. The sailboat was wonderful for entertaining, but it was not readily accessible. James had learned long ago that familiarity breeds contempt, so he never invited the politicians or other lobbyists on weekend sails. A sunset cocktail sail was as close as he wanted to get to them. James thought, like Kimberly, that it was best to keep his legislative and political life separate from his personal friends.

James was a member of the small yacht club at the lake. It wasn't a prestigious yacht club like Kimberly had seen many times before. It was a bunch of good folks who enjoyed the other sailors and sailed their small sailboats. Occasionally there were parties, but nothing like Kimberly had seen when she had attended the America's Cup. The club was made up of local folks who just enjoyed getting away. James did not know many of the members, but those he knew liked him.

When James picked up Kimberly at her condo, she looked like a model in a Ralph Lauren catalog. She certainly knew how to dress for sailing.

"You will be the prettiest woman who ever sailed on my sailboat."

"Good. I read a book about sailing one time," Kimberly said.

"You're absolutely beautiful. Would you be my sailorette?"

"Well, I would like to be your sailorette." They both laughed, and Kimberly fastened her seat belt as James drove off.

As James drove toward the lake, they listened to the music and talked about work. James played Jimmy Buffett songs, and Kimberly enjoyed them. During one of the songs, they sang along with the CD. When they arrived, James unloaded a cooler and placed it in the cockpit of the boat. He unlocked the cabin and stepped inside. He opened the windows and hatches to allow air to circulate in the cabin.

Kimberly was still standing on the wharf. "Permission to come aboard, Captain?"

James stood up, extended his hand, and replied, "Permission granted. Welcome aboard the *Liberty*."

He had bought the boat from an estate sale and was told by the widow that her husband had crossed the Atlantic in it. The boat was in immaculate condition. It looked like it had just come out of the factory.

James checked the engine oil to be certain it was OK. He started the small inboard diesel engine and allowed it to run for a few minutes while they got the cushions out of the cabin for the cockpit. The jib was equipped with roller furling and would roll out easily, but the mainsail had to be lifted into position. James removed the cover on the mainsail and asked Kimberly to help him remove the lines from the dock. He put the engine in reverse and backed out of the slip.

"To sea we go!" James announced.

Just beyond the harbor, he raised the mainsail and rolled out the jib while Kimberly steered the boat. The afternoon was beautiful, and the winds were perfect. James had recently added an autopilot to the boat. He turned the autopilot on and set it to sail to the island in the middle of the lake. The sail was perfect. The winds were not heavy, and the lake was not rough.

James lowered the sails about one hundred feet from the island and dropped the anchor. Then, in his tux T-shirt, he said, "Would you like to have a glass of wine, Miss Kimberly?"

"Yes, sir, Captain James."

"The captain is serving white or red. Which one would you prefer?"

"Red," Kimberly said. As the boat moved lightly with the waves, they drank the wine, ate the nibbles, and watched the sunset. The sun looked like a huge red ball dropping over the horizon. It was falling so fast, they could see the movement.

"This must be the most beautiful place in the world," Kimberly said.

"It's probably in the top five," James laughed and said, "but it depends on who you're with."

On the foredeck James leaned back against the cabin, and Kimberly laid her head on his chest. After finishing the wine, they made love in the forward cabin. The cabin had a V-berth large enough for two people. They lay in the cabin as the boat rocked with the water for an hour or more.

They had not realized it was dark outside. When James noticed the dark, he said, "We need to head for shore. We both have a busy day tomorrow."

"I don't want to go. I want to stay here the rest of my life and hold you in my arms forever."

"Come on, gorgeous, the wind is off the starboard side, and we should have a perfect sail back to the harbor." He was right. The moon had appeared, and the wind was perfect, eight knots or so. The moon sparkled on the water like diamonds had been dropped from the sky. The reflection of the moon diamonds was mesmerizing. James turned on the autopilot, and they moved the cockpit cushions to the foredeck. From there the lake water sounded like a relaxing song as it splashed against the bow. In the distance they could see the harbor lights.

"This is the most perfect evening of my life. I love you, James. When are you going to marry me?" Kimberly said.

James acted as if he didn't hear the question and said, "Those harbor lights are beautiful."

"I know what you're doing. You're changing the subject. You're not going to be able to avoid the answer forever. You never know, I might withdraw the question. The problem is, I won't, and you know it because I love you so much."

At the dock they secured the boat and departed for the city, talking and laughing and smiling all the way.

OLD SENATOR EXPLAINS TRUCK LAWS

As Mike and James entered his office, Senator Jackson said, "Good morning, boys. It's Mike and James, correct?"

Both James and Mike replied, "Yes, sir."

"I understand you boys need some counseling. You've come to the right man. I hear Senator Blackman and Representative Todd have introduced a bill to lower the speeds on your trucks and reduce the weights they can carry, is that right?"

"Yes, sir, Senator."

"Since the damn old whores are not around, we can get down to some serious business. I'll educate you boys, if you would like," he said.

"Thank you, Senator," James said. "You know we are beginners, and your help will be appreciated."

"First, did you boys get Jones and Todd to introduce the bills?"

"No, it's an administration bill," James said.

"It would have been better if you had, because then you could have killed it. However, if your clients caught you doing that, you certainly would get fired. I'll bet you that truck speeds are a much deeper issue than you boys realize. If I'm correct, and I'm sure I am, don't feel like you're alone. Many, if not most, legislators who vote on raising and lowering truck speeds never realize the underlying forces that are at play. The same is true for truck weights. Fuck, they don't realize the issue has a large impact on the cost of labor and merchandise purchased by the good people of the state," Senator Jackson explained.

The senator asked James, "Did you know that?"

"To be perfectly honest, I never thought about it."

"Nor has the public thought about it," the senator said, as he leaned back in his chair and placed his cowboy boots on top of the desk. "That's in your favor, son, because you can tell just one side of the story. The public is on its own. Remember, them goddamn bureaucrats don't give a shit, and that's to your advantage also."

James started to comment, but before he could say anything, the senator said, "Boys, let me give you an example. Assume a trucking company is hauling five tons of material from the northern part of the state to the southern part of the state, and state law allows a truck to haul all five tons in one trip. This requires hiring only one driver and using one truck.

"The total cost would be more if a truck could haul only four tons. For the other ton of material, the company would have to hire another driver and use a second truck. Drivers and trucks are expensive. If the trucks were rolling every day year-round, the cost to the company would be astronomical.

Therefore, you boys as lobbyists certainly want a state law that would allow the truck company to make only one trip rather than two."

Mike's mind wandered back to Donald in the coffee shop and the soccer moms that morning as the senator talked. Just before going to the senator's office, Mike and James had listened to Donald explain the funkily dressed housewives who he referred to as legislative whores.

Donald had stopped the conversation by saying, "Hold it right there, boys, I need to go see that chick over there by the elevator." He left the table and walked fast to catch the blond, well-endowed woman waiting for the elevator. James and Mike had watched Donald through the glass wall of the coffee shop as he talked to the woman. She was dressed in a short skirt and boots, with her breasts almost completely exposed. They could tell she was certainly not a Sunday school teacher.

After about five minutes, Donald returned to the table with a smile on his face and said, "There are several like her. She's a married soccer mom who changes clothes after dropping off the kids for school and shows up each session of the legislature looking for a new lay with an expense account. They are legislative whores. When the legislature is in town, good and loving housewives like her show up. Have you noticed how many big-breasted women are around here since the legislature arrived in town? I'm going to fuck her later over at her house on Lakeshore Drive. Her husband is a big-time doctor. She loves to fuck and provides some cocaine and a joint or two to enhance the experience a little bit. She likes fancy trick fucking. I'm going to meet her today at three o'clock. You boys want to come along? She and that girl she's talking to now will take on all three of us for a little afternoon delight."

Mike and James both said no instantly.

"That bitch is screwing Senator Abraham and Representative Calendar once a week," Donald laughed. "She says Abraham's looks like a pencil."

The senator noticed that Mike's mind was somewhere else. "Wake up, Mike. Am I boring you?"

"No, sir. I was just thinking about what you said."

Then the old senator continued. "To a large trucking company, the number of trips could mean millions of dollars. To an independent trucker you represent, it could mean food on the table. To you boys and me, it means making a little money. For me as a senator, the trucking companies come to see me and donate a few dollars to my campaign every year. For that they hope I will stamp out the Department of Transportation. Of course, I'm not going to try to do that, because then they wouldn't come contribute to my campaign. Plus, you boys wouldn't play poker with me, and if you did, you'd probably win every time. What a great system we have. You agree?" Both Mike and James nodded their heads yes.

"You boys likely have seen things differently. You viewed trucks like others, especially heavy trucks, as breaking the highways, and there's some truth to that. I bet you thought the heavier the truck, the shorter the life of the highways. The highway section of the department is charged with protecting the roadways, but I bet you never thought they had to confront trucking lobbyists like you two fine young men.

"In summary, you boys need to realize that the public wants lightweight trucks that travel at slow speeds. Trucking companies want trucks to be loaded as heavy as possible and to travel at a reasonably high speed. From you boys' point of view as lobbyists for truckers, it's a good thing the public doesn't have paid lobbyists. Their lobbyists are the Transportation Department bureaucrats. Most of those motherfuckers are laissez-faire political appointees and only want to draw a paycheck anyway. They don't really give a shit about truck weight or speed, but they're forced to pretend they do," he said, as he took his cowboy boots off his desk and leaned forward. "I hope you boys didn't mind me putting my shit kickers on my desk."

Mike responded, "No, sir," and James nodded his head in agreement.

"I understand you represent two kinds of trucks, independent truckers and ready-mixed concrete trucks," the senator continued. "The way I see it, in most cases each has a slightly different interest but overall are united. Isn't that correct?"

"Yes. There certainly is not a conflict of interest," Mike said.

The senator then said, "There's another lobbyist representing the cross-country truckers. He generally doesn't understand what's going on. That silly bastard won't even accept my invitation to play poker. Some say he's in bed with the bureaucrats at the department. The truckers will fire him someday. If they ever talk to me about him, they certainly will. He is damn sure a high-pockets asshole.

"Now, boys, if the concrete producers haven't told you, I'll tell you. Weight laws are critical to concrete companies. If you allow a bill to pass that lowers the weight on concrete trucks, I'm certain they will fire you. These laws determine the number of yards of concrete a ready-mix truck can carry to a job. If a job requires nine yards of concrete, and state law permits nine, then one driver could make one trip. If state law requires no more than six yards of concrete, then the delivery requires two drivers and two trips. Most concrete truck drivers belong to the Teamsters Union, and they are not cheap labor."

About that time the old senator's secretary, Ethel, walked into the office and told him that he had a committee hearing coming up in a few minutes. After she left the room he said, "That old girl loves me. I've gotten every one of her family a lucrative state contract or a job. I know I could get some of that, but I don't screw the help."

He continued, "It's your job to draft and pass state laws that will allow ready-mix trucks to carry as many yards as is reasonably possible. The goddamn speed is not that important to concrete trucks because most operate in the cities. I have four concrete producers in my district, and they all are good friends of mine. I will vote whichever way they want me to. They are good contributors and supporters of mine.

"If you haven't realized it yet, loyalty to those who help you is the key word around this place. The second thing you need to remember is the golden rule, which I am certain you have heard before. Those who have the gold make the rules. Now, boys, if you get in trouble, call me. I'm the man you need to know when you're in trouble. Oh, by the way, I appreciate you playing poker with me. I have a very busy schedule today, but there is one other thing I want to tell you boys. I hope you guys don't mind me calling you boys."

They laughed and then James said, "No, sir, Senator."

"OK, then let's talk about killing unfavorable bills, boys. That's where you can appear to be powerful. You see, most people don't know that it's easier to kill a bill than to pass a bill. So when you kill a bill, everyone you represent thinks you are great. As the lobbyist for truckers and concrete, a major part of your job is to kill any unfavorable bills. Year after year the Department of Transportation will draft laws to reduce the yardage, and year after year you can kill the bills. It's a win-win situation for you boys.

"You tell every representative and senator that the concrete industry leadership realizes it is not to their advantage to break highways. They are for reasonable weight laws and other ways of protecting the highways. Point out to them that the balloon tires used by ready-mix trucks spread the weight on the roadbed and reduce damage. If it looks like you're losing, you should suggest that concrete producers might consider implementing retractable third or fourth rear axles that can be lowered when the truck is loaded. This also will reduce the pressure on the roadbed. In other words, the concrete industry isn't a group of cowboys trying to break up the highways with no regard to the public interest. They are responsible citizens who want reasonable weight laws. Am I going too fast for you boys? You're welcome to take notes. It won't bother me.

"I know the independent truckers have told you the truckers who haul across the state are also interested in higher weights. That's because they are generally paid based on the amount of product they deliver. If state law limits their truck weight to sixty thousand pounds per truck, then the truck could not carry as much product as it could if the limit were eighty thousand pounds. Also, as I mentioned earlier, lower speeds mean fewer deliveries and therefore less income for the independent trucker. I know you've heard this before; it's all about money."

Mike and James simultaneously shook their heads yes.

"In years past I've heard the independent truckers argue that their trucks travel faster and don't pressure the roadbed as much as slow trucks. There's some truth to that. You boys might have noticed that many times the roadbeds are broken in the last two or three hundred yards of an intersection or where a large number of trucks enter the highway. I'm told by some state employees the reason the last section of the highway breaks is because if the state is building one hundred miles of road, by the time they get to the last five miles, the contractors have gotten too friendly with the inspectors. With all that said, I hope you're getting an understanding of the system."

James and Mike nodded their heads and said yes.

"Again, the good news for you boys is that bills dealing with weight laws generally don't make the newspaper even though they have a tremendous impact on the economy. Remember, when the cost of delivering products increases, the product cost increases, and the public pays. When the roadbeds are broken, the public pays. You boys remember the old saying used a lot around here, 'When the legislature is in session, no man's wallet is safe.' That includes yours. Sorry, boys, but I must go now. I have a committee meeting starting in five minutes." Then he picked up a lawbook and held it up so Mike and James could see it. He said as he walked out of the office with the GOB following him, "Many of the laws in this book were passed with most of the members of the legislature not understanding what they were really about or what was going on behind the scenes."

Mike and James thanked the senator. They told him that he had been very helpful and they appreciated it and that when he had a vacant space at his poker table, they wanted to play again.

"Don't worry, boys, I'll be calling on you. Now remember, if you get in trouble, I'm the man you need to call. Don't forget, boys, the key word here is loyalty, loyalty, and loyalty to those who help you."

Mike and James left the senator's office and walked down the hallway and out to the parking lot where Mike's car was parked. On the way to the car, James told Mike, "I'm amazed. I thought he was just an old womanizing drunk, but he knows some shit. My God, how could he know so much about such a small area of the law?"

"He's been around twenty years," Mike said.

"We need to keep him on our side," James said.

"You're damn right," Mike agreed.

James looked at him and said, "Mike, do you realize how many areas of law we don't know shit about?"

"Yes," Mike replied.

They both realized they had a lot of learning to do, and they had to do it fast. Mike said, "I'm going to call it a day and go home. See you at seven in the morning."

NEED POKING

Back at the Greenhouse, James called Kimberly to tell her about the meeting with the senator.

She said, "That's great. He likes you. It's unusual for him to do something like that. You're going to have to keep playing poker." Then she said, "Talking about poker, you haven't done any poking lately."

"Well, I'll have to take care of that. Where would you like to meet?"

"How about the Cellar Bar?"

"OK, five o'clock. See you there," she said.

When they walked in, the German started mixing two martinis. They were up and dirty. He swirled vermouth around the interior of the glasses while ice chilled them. Then the vermouth and ice were poured out. Vodka was poured into the stemmed martini glasses with a German flag etched in the side. He added two olives on a stick and olive juice to make the drinks dirty. Then he placed the drinks on the oxidized copper bar. Old wine bottles that had not been cleaned in years hung on each end of the small bar, and wineglasses hung overhead like bowling pins.

With a smile and a thank you, they picked up the drinks and took them to their usual corner table. James expounded on what the senator had said while they sipped their martinis. Kimberly listened. Then he told her about Donald and the married woman.

"You need to be careful around Donald," she said. "He's known as a womanizer and known for dirty tricks and drugs. He's smart and can be very helpful to you, and he's a genius in parliamentary procedure. It's interesting that he's trying to help you because he usually keeps to himself and a very small group of lobbyist friends. He only works with those he can use. I suppose he thinks he can use you in the future." An hour had passed, and they were still talking.

"Let me tell you a secret. Lean forward," James whispered. They both leaned forward, and he said, "I need to do some poking."

"That sounds good. I've missed your poker."

He kissed her across the small table. "Your place or mine?" he said.

"Mine. See you there," she said.

Upon arrival she handed James a gift-wrapped package and said, "I got you something."

"What is it? You shouldn't have bought me anything."

"Open it and be quiet. I can do whatever I want."

He opened the gift with his usual slow technique. Inside he found a beautiful and very expensive-looking dress shirt. He examined it carefully and said, "This will be the best shirt I own."

"That's good—you will think of me every time you wear it."

He put his arm around her, and they kissed as if the world was ending and it would be their last kiss. She took his hand and led him to her bed. The bed was absolutely gorgeous. It was covered completely with Ralph Lauren bedding, with a multitude of pillows of various colors and shapes. While standing beside the bed, they undressed each other as if they had to be naked in five seconds or life would end. Their lovemaking seemed to get more and more intense each time. Neither had ever experienced so much passion.

After sex they talked about the capitol, the people in her office, the governor, and so forth.

Then she said, "You stay right here. I have a surprise for you."

"Oh, not another gift," he said.

"Be quiet and stay put." She went into the bathroom, and after a few minutes returned. She put her still-nude body over his as he lay on his back, the way she had left him.

"What are you up to?" he asked.

"It's a surprise," she whispered in his ear. After a few minutes, he could smell an aroma coming from the bathroom. He asked what that nice smell was.

She pulled him by the hand while at the same time saying, "Come with me and you will see." When he walked into the bathroom, he couldn't believe how big it was. He thought it was about four times the size of his apartment bedroom. Before, he had only been in the small bathroom off of another bedroom. This bathroom looked like a church altar. Beautiful candles of all sizes surrounded the bathtub. The aroma was overwhelming and wonderful.

"Would you like to take a bubble bath with me?" she asked. The large tub was almost overflowing with bubbles.

James answered, "Yes, I think I would like to take a bubble bath with you." He got into the tub first. Then she entered, being careful not to touch one of the candles on the way. After a few minutes of small talk, he wrapped his arms around her, holding both of her breasts. She reached around her body, touching him, and soon they were making love in the tub. It was like an animal instinct that was uncontrollable.

James felt guilty because he had planned not to become involved with anyone for a long period after his divorce, but the temptation was just too great. Plus, she was helping him start Good Ole Boys and Associates. She was advising and encouraging him daily, sometimes almost hourly. He just didn't realize how much she was helping. He had no idea that her father had gotten him two of his major clients. He had no concept as to how rich she was. At first he thought she was just another average-pay state employee, but the condo did not add up. Even with the deal she said she had gotten on it, she obviously couldn't afford it as a state employee. Maybe she had inherited it, or maybe her parents were helping her. James didn't want to be nosey about her personal business, so he didn't ask.

CHAPTER 9

BECOMING AN INSIDER

BLUE SKIES IN ITALY

James told Kimberly he was having someone over for dinner at his apartment.

Kimberly asked, "Who is it?"

"It's a surprise. I plan to cook, but I need to buy the ingredients. Would you help me shop? The dinner is Saturday, and the legislature is adjourned for the weekend."

"Yes, that would be fun," Kimberly said. "We will go to Whole Foods."

"No, that's too expensive. Let's go to one of the more common grocery stores. It's not like I'm trying to wine and dine these people. Only one of them is important to me, and that's you. I don't have to shop at Whole Foods to impress you."

"James, you are just a tightwad."

"That's correct, but I prefer to be called frugal." They laughed. "What are your favorite appetizer, main course, and dessert?"

"Oh, you know I only eat fish. Other than that I'm almost a vegetarian."

"OK, a Caesar salad and trout for the main dish," James said.

"You forgot the appetizer."

"What do you suggest?"

"How about bruschetta on slices of toasted baguette for the appetizer? The dessert could be peaches with yogurt on top."

"Maybe some ice cream. If there's any left over, I can keep it in my freezer."

"We will need to make a grocery list and go shopping on Friday after work."

"OK, I'll meet you at my apartment at five thirty."

Friday evening James and Kimberly went to a large food store to buy the groceries on Kimberly's list. She said, "The shopping is more fun than the dinner."

"Maybe. Wait and see." They took the food to James's apartment. At the apartment they made love.

"Kimberly, spend the night with me," and she did. The next morning after making love they showered. Then they started preparing the dinner for that night.

"I can finish this. You go home, and I will take care of the rest," James told Kimberly.

"OK, see you at seven."

When Kimberly returned at seven, she was amazed. The table was covered with a very pretty tablecloth and neatly folded cloth napkins. There were beautiful flowers and lit candles in the center of the table. The silverware and china were stunning. The table was set for two.

She looked and looked and thought. Finally, as James waited anxiously to hear her remarks, she said, "Who did all this? Where are the others going to sit?"

"There are no others," James said. "It's just the two of us. I wanted to spend the day with you, and I didn't want to ask you what you wanted to eat, so I let you help me select the food. It was fun shopping with you. I wanted to surprise you. Did I?"

She walked across the room, kissed him, and said, "You are the most wonderful man I've ever known. I'm going to marry you."

"Oh, maybe someday. Let's not move too fast."

She smiled and laughed to herself. *Maybe.*

He pulled a chair out from the table for her to have a seat. Then he went to the kitchen, brought out the appetizers, and took a seat across from her at the table.

A few minutes later, James said, "Oh, I forgot I gave the servants the day off." He went to the kitchen and returned with the salad.

After the salad, James brought out the rest of the meal as the time came for it. After the meal was completed, James brought out a gift-wrapped box about ten inches long, four inches wide, and one inch thick, with a beautiful, colorful bow on it.

He told her, "You will be surprised, but I finally found something I know you don't have."

She started opening the gift-wrapped box, tearing the paper off as rapidly as she could to see what was inside. There were two airplane tickets and hotel reservations for a small, romantic hotel in Rome and another in Venice. James didn't know it at the time, but this gift was going to change his life forever.

"I apologize for making the assumption that you would consider traveling with me," he said.

"You made a great decision. I can't wait. When are we going?" She looked at the tickets and said, "September after the session. That's great. I've never been to Italy. I have read that Rome is a beautiful, wonderful, romantic city. I understand Venice is even better. Do we have to wait until September?"

"Yes, be patient, young lady."

She came around the table to James and said, "I love you."

"Love is a serious word," he said.

"I understand that, and I'm crazy in love with you."

"I sort of like you too," James said.

"You better, because I'm going to marry you."

James picked her up and carried her to the bedroom. "We're going to wear out this bed, if it's not already worn out."

"Good, we can always get another one. Now shut up and please make love to me."

The next day was Sunday, and they stayed in bed all day watching old television movies and eating snacks.

WEIGHT WATCHERS DIET FOR TRUCKS

Mike and James had done everything Donald had told them to do to kill a bill. Mike wanted to do one other thing. On the day of the hearing, the leaders of concrete met in a room on the first floor of the state capitol. Old Senator Jackson had arranged for them to have a private meeting room at the capitol. Mike and James had developed a handout with a list of talking points for those who would testify or speak to a legislator before the hearing.

They suggested that each person talk to some of the representatives. They explained how to call them off the floor of the house or senate to the side rail for a conversation about the bill. They did not tell the leaders which legislators were going to vote for them or which ones they thought were going to vote against them. From the vote count Mike and James had calculated, they were going to win eight to three, but they did not tell the group because they wanted the leaders to hustle every legislator.

James walked the concrete group to the committee room where they would testify at eleven o'clock, while Mike met with independent truckers on the top floor in another room that had been arranged by Senator Jackson.

James told Mike, "We really owe Senator Jackson. The groups are impressed that we could get a room set aside just for them in the state capitol." Mike agreed by nodding his head. The Truckers Association president and five other independent truckers met with Mike. Mike covered the same items the James had reviewed with the concrete producers. He walked them to the second floor to see the committee room and then sent them on their way to hustle votes.

If someone wanted to testify, the rules required that every person complete the form requesting permission to speak before the committee. On the form one must indicate whether he was for or against the bill. Kimberly told James to tell Mike to have each person complete the Request to

Testify form so it would appear to the committee members that many people were against the bill. Mike thought that was a great idea, and he made sure everyone completed the form listing the company represented and the bill he wanted to defeat.

When the meeting started, fifteen people were against the bill, and only the Department of Transportation staffers were for it.

The chairman of the committee said, "There are so many people against this bill, could we have just one representative of the concrete industry and one representative of the truckers testify on behalf of all?"

James was already at the table. He turned and invited the presidents to join him. James started the testimony by saying the bill would do nothing for the highways, but it would damage the business of truckers and concrete for years to come. He pointed out that it would raise the price of consumer items. James continued talking and noting other problems with the bill. He was such a smooth talker that everyone in the room wanted to vote to kill the bill before hearing anyone else's testimony. James had found he was extremely good at testifying. It was like he was born to testify before committees.

The committee chairman said, "James, that was an excellent presentation." To have a committee chairperson make such a remark was extremely unusual.

After the Department of Transportation staffers testified, the chairman called for the vote. James and Mike won, nine to two. One of them who had told James and Mike he was voting against them changed his mind after seeing the group of truckers and concrete producers.

The group went to the Greenhouse for lunch. During lunch they met with some of the legislators and thanked them for their vote. As the president of the Concrete Association left, he told James and Mike they were doing a wonderful job. He thought they deserved a little bonus at the end of the session. He said he would talk to the board of directors about it.

BIG BOYS WITH BIG MONEY

The president of the Concrete Association called Mike and told him there was a meeting every Monday morning of the State Business and Manufacturing Association. The meeting was by invitation only. He told Mike the president of the association had invited him and James to attend. They should be at the association headquarters Monday morning at seven. Mike agreed to attend but did not know what they were getting into.

On Monday at seven o'clock, as directed, the boys attended the meeting. It was a large conference room with twenty or thirty chairs and a speaker's podium up front. The participants represented almost all Fortune 500 businesses that James and Mike knew of in the state. People from big manufacturing companies to retailers were in the meeting. These were certainly the heavy hitters of big business. Later, a tall slim man with red hair who was definitely in control came in and went directly to the podium. Both James and Mike recognized him from television news conferences. He was the man everyone wanted to talk to about one thing or another on opening day. He introduced James and Mike to everyone in the room and told them they represented concrete.

The agenda included much bigger items than Mike and James would likely be lobbying for or against. Everything from educational reform, liability reform, property tax, and environmental issues were on the schedule. The commercial construction lobbyists were there in force. Donald and some of the other lobbyists they had met, such as Paul and Bobby, were not in attendance.

After the meeting was over, the tall man called Mike and James to the front of the room and told them, "Welcome." Then he pointed out to them that attendance was by invitation only and that topics covered were confidential. They were not to bring any other lobbyists with them. They could bring a client, but it had to be preapproved.

Several of the Fortune 500, 400, and 300 lobbyists came to Mike and James after the meeting to welcome them. It was like they had been accepted into a very selective club. Most offered to help them with any issues if they needed it. Several gave them business cards and said things like let's keep in touch or see you next Monday.

Some things were confusing to Mike and James. During the meeting, educational reform was a big part of the discussion. The agenda was mostly about how to demand teacher accountability and how to cut off funds to the teachers' unions and other educational funding. Each large company was assigned a group of legislators to meet with about killing the unions' impact.

The next issue was property tax. They wanted to shift the burden of taxes on business and manufacturing over to the homeowners in the state.

"We have the power and can totally eliminate property taxes our companies pay," said one of the Fortune 500 company lobbyists.

The redheaded leader of the group immediately spoke. "No, we must be responsible corporate citizens. The state needs roads, buildings, employees, and schools. The companies we represent must pay their fair share." Looking at the lobbyist who had made the remark he said, "Pigs get fat and hogs get slaughtered. We would be fools to abuse our power. Political power is always temporary. It's like a pendulum: when it swings too far to one side it comes back fast and hard. So let's pay our fair share." His remark was made like a mother scolding a greedy child. Then he moved on to other subjects.

These were huge issues, ones James and Mike were not a part of and probably didn't want to be.

Then the tall man said he was going to have a news conference on educational reform that day. That afternoon Mike and James attended the news conference in the state capitol. To their surprise the news conference was very different from the morning meeting. The tall man said he wanted to get along with the teachers and their unions and wanted to see that education was adequately funded so all children in the state got a good education. At the same time, those large company lobbyists were working the committees to cut the budgets for public education and to provide funding to schools owned by businesses, as instructed that morning. In other words, what the public was seeing on television was not what was happening behind the scenes.

James and Mike looked at each other, and Mike said, "Oh, my God! Who would ever think that what you see on television is so different from what goes on in real time?"

It seemed that every day, a new world of disbelief opened up to the Good Ole Boys. They began to realize there was more to it than just two bullshitters bullshitting the bullshitters, as they had thought in the beginning. It was real power and money. It was big banks, big oil, big chemicals, and big retailers battling the big unions and the public. It was a serious game, and many times the details were undisclosed.

KEEP AN EYE ON THOSE GUYS

Like any other business, a lobbyist has to keep an eye on the competition. Lobbyists must identify those businesses that have an interest in passing laws that would give their clients' business an advantage over others. General contractors were the group that James and Mike had to watch, especially when it came to lien laws.

These laws determined the method and time in which contractors, subcontractors, materials suppliers, and others could file a lien against a property for nonpayment. Concrete was the first and the largest supplier to grant credit to the contractor on most construction jobs. The invoice generally gave the contractor thirty days to pay. Some offered the contractor a 5 percent discount if paid on time. When the contractor failed to take the 5 percent, the concrete supplier knew something was wrong. Then the concrete supplier's option was to file a lien to preserve his right of collection. In other words, a property could not be sold without removing the lien, and the concrete dealer had control of the release button. The lien also alerted the building materials dealers, whom James and Mike also represented, to the fact that the contractor was not paying on time.

When a concrete supplier filed a lien, it often shut down the construction job. The law allowed sixty days for the supplier to file a lien. The concrete supplier did not want to file a lien, if possible. The contractor might simply be having a cash flow problem, and if the concrete supplier filed a lien, it would anger the contractor. The contractor would likely never buy concrete from them again. The lien laws gave concrete a real advantage over the construction industry. But it was an advantage they did not want to use or lose.

Lien laws became a contentious issue between suppliers and contractors, especially concrete. Contractors were constantly trying to increase the time permitted before a lien could be filed against them so that concrete companies, if they were not watching their construction customers, would lose their advantage. Concrete constantly wanted to decrease the time. With issues like this in play and as the lobbyists for the concrete industry, James and Mike constantly had to watch the construction lobbyist. Any time they went into a committee hearing, they followed or looked at the agenda to see if there were issues they needed to watch. Generally, concrete was on the same side as the contractors, but there were areas where there were differences. Lien laws were just one example.

LOBBYING POSITION WITH FORTUNE 400 COMPANY

"I was offered a job lobbying for a Fortune 400 company yesterday, but I would have to become a full-time employee of the company and lobby for no one else," James told Mike at breakfast.

"Really," Mike said.

"I told them about our services and tried to convince them to let the GOB represent them. They would not consider GOB. It wouldn't make any sense for me to go to work for them. I would get an excellent salary and have an expense account, but I would be back to what I hated—working for someone else. Plus, I could never make as much money working for them as I can with you and GOB."

"Well, I'm glad you're not leaving GOB," Mike said.

"Corporate lobbyists are just employees of big corporations, and you would have only one client, the corporation. If something goes wrong with that one client, you're out of a job and out of lobbying. The GOB would have to get fired by several groups before we would be out of lobbying," James said.

"Plus, when someone on the board of directors of the corporation wants his brother-in-law to be the company's lobbyist, you're out of a job and on the street," Mike said.

James nodded his head. "Yes," he said, "you're right, and that's why I would not consider leaving the GOB for a job as a company lobbyist. Everyone in this business gets fired by clients at sometime or another."

WHY DIDN'T I THINK OF THAT?

Mike noticed the construction lobbyists going into the Criminal Justice Committee hearings. He and James couldn't figure out what their interests could be, so they asked one of the construction lobbyists. He gave James and Mike a strange answer. He said they were just interested in criminal justice. Knowing that contractors had other important issues, they

John O. Murphy Ed.D.

couldn't imagine the construction lobbyists attending a committee hearing just because they were "interested." They knew something was up but couldn't figure out what it was.

A past president of the statewide Contractors Association was a personal friend of Mike's. He and Mike had lunch together frequently. Mike told him about the construction lobbyist and the Criminal Justice Committee and asked him what their interest might be. His answer was simple.

"They were trying to make certain that criminals got long sentences."

"Why would they be interested in that?" Mike asked.

"Contractors get to build the jails. Longer sentences mean more jails are needed," he said with a laugh.

Mike wondered why he hadn't thought of that. It was all about the "money pie" and how it was divided.

The way Mike and James thought about issues and life was changing. They had learned there are many issues like this in the legislature. A lobbyist had to look at every side and all possibilities without emotions. After a period of time, a lobbyist's mind never worked the same again. He was always wondering what the politics were behind all issues.

Mike's friend also pointed out that they wanted to make certain the criminals were not allowed to do any work outside the prison, especially construction work. If prison labor was used, a contractor didn't get to build a building or remodel a facility. He said prisoners could be used to do state construction projects, build highways, and maintain state buildings. The contractor would be replaced and save the state money. Some said it would help rehabilitate prisoners, but the contractors were not interested in rehabilitating the prisoners. They were interested in construction jobs that required a general contractor. The lobbyist for the contractors didn't represent the prisoners. He represented the contractors.

AGGREGATES—WHAT IS THAT?

While James was visiting with the concrete producers, the president told him that the gravel mining companies would like to meet with the GOB to talk about being represented by them. He told James they liked to be called aggregate suppliers—nothing more than a fancy word for fucking rocks. James took the number of the gentleman he needed to call. During his drive back to the capital city, he called Mr. Wilson from his new cellular phone. James told him who he was and who recommended that he call him. Mr. Wilson thanked him for calling and said they needed someone like him. Then Mr. Wilson asked where he was at that moment. James said he had just passed exit number fifty on the interstate. Mr. Wilson told him to take exit number fifty-eight, turn left, and drive two miles straight ahead to the dead end. He would be at his gravel pit. James told him he would be there in a few minutes.

Mr. Wilson and James met for an hour, and he agreed to hire James and Mike. James told him the fee would be $135,000 per year. Plus, there would be a 20 percent entertainment fee. James showed him a stack of fund-raising invitations his office received each year that the GOB would have to attend.

"That is a lot of money, but I think I can raise it in a couple of weeks," Mr. Wilson said.

Two weeks later, Mr. Wilson called and said he was coming into the city to give the boys a check. James suggested they meet at the Greenhouse to sign the contract. James also suggested a day when he knew the legislative Budget Committee was meeting so senators and representatives would be in the Greenhouse having lunch.

Mr. Wilson arrived on the planned date about noon, and senators and representatives were already starting to gather in the Greenhouse. Mr. Wilson engaged in conversation with several representatives and afterward had no problem whatsoever giving the boys a check for half of the $135,000 and another check for entertainment purposes. He signed the contract for the list of gravel producers he had gotten together. The contract read that the other half of the $135,000 was due in six months. Again, the Greenhouse was used to impress potential clients.

During the meeting, James and Mike asked Mr. Wilson what potential legislation they would be interested in. Mr. Wilson said to watch the Clean Rivers Act. He told them about a hearing next week that they should attend to see if it would affect gravel. James and Mike assured him they would be in the hearing. If gravel were included in the act, then gravel as they knew it would be out of the river, and that could put them out of business. Mr. Wilson said they did not want government involved in their business whatsoever, no matter how small the issue.

GOB and Associates had another client, and they were moving on. It seemed that one good client always led to another good client.

BROAD-BASED ISSUES

At the state capitol, the executive director of the state Forestry Association approached James. His name was Eddie.

He asked James if he and Mike would help with the reform of the state's workers' compensation laws. The word *reform* generally meant to change the law to favor the reformer and had nothing to do with good government.

"What do you expect of us?" James asked.

Eddie explained to Mike and James the importance of workers' comp laws and what they cost the businesses the two of them represented.

Mike said he would pass it by their clients and ask what they would like to do. Mike called the president of the Concrete Association and discussed workers' compensation laws.

The Good Ole Boys had already realized they needed to define the scope of the issues they should become involved with. Each law or issue consumed time and money. Donald and Paul had told them broad-based issues should be left to broad-based organizations. By broad-based organizations, they meant, for example, manufacturing associations, business associations, and unions.

The GOB went to talk to Donald about the Forestry Association's request. Donald said, "Associations such as forestry have many issues to deal with other than workers' comp laws. They range from laws related to clear-cutting to tree huggers, and so forth. He needs to focus on those. You tell him thanks, but no thanks. Workers' compensation is an issue for broad-based organizations such as the statewide association of business and manufacturing. Point out to him that you need to focus on specific issues that have a specific impact on your clients. Workers' comp laws do affect your clients, but they also affect a large number, if not all, of other businesses. Then tell him maybe you can help him next year. Between me and you, I predict he likely will not be around next year."

The forestry guy did not like Mike and James's answer to his request, but as James theorized, "He will get over it. We can't please everybody."

During the legislative session, the forestry lobbyist spent hours and hours and hours working on workers' comp laws. He was the hero of the statewide Business Association, but he became a target of the labor unions. He had become a servant of the Business Association.

After the session was over, the unions set out to get him fired by the Forestry Association. The unions threaten to unionize certain timber companies if they did not fire Eddie. The timber companies that put large sums of money into the Forestry Association got the board of directors to fire Eddie immediately. It was simple: deal with a union organizer or fire Eddie. Eddie was fired. The statewide business organization did not come to his rescue. They had just used him.

THE WEBSITE

Nan, the student Mike and James had hired to do clerical work and answer the phone, told them she had been observing what they were doing and had developed a website to help them. She said, "I haven't published it on the web yet because I wanted to get your approval. Would you like to look at it?"

Both Mike and James simultaneously said, "Yes, let's see it." She typed the web domain name she had purchased, and sure enough, there was a beautiful website showing pictures of Mike and James, with the goals and objectives of their lobbying firm. It made them look like angels who had been successful for years.

Mike and James couldn't believe it. Nan was turning out to be very valuable. She also pointed out that they could enter the names of their clients and do mass mailings easily and therefore eliminate Phyllis. Mike reached in his pocket and pulled out two one-hundred-dollar bills.

He handed them to Nan and said, "Go treat yourself to something special. Make the site live on the web immediately. Also, we are raising your pay fifty dollars a week. You should start entering the database and make the website you created the digital manager of our business."

They had not seen any other lobbyists on the web in their state. After seeing what Nan did, they wondered why no one had at least a web page.

"I think it is the nature of the business," James said. "Remember, this is bullshitters bullshitting bullshitters. Most of them are not technologically advanced. This website will help us secure more clients. I'm going to call some legislative staffers and see what they think about it."

What James meant was he was going to call Kimberly. He told her the web domain name and asked her to look at the site on her computer. She did and said, "Wonderful; that looks great. That must have cost you a pretty penny."

"No, the university student in our office did it. She's a computer technology major. We're going to be able to use this site to contact clients and to manage our office."

INSIDER TRADING

A large company that had been recklessly polluting the air and water and was predicted to be shut down by the environmental agency was arguing to keep its operational permit.

James and Mike were sitting in the meeting as instructed by Mr. Wilson. There was another item on the agenda that could affect the sand and gravel people, but it was tabled. To the surprise of everyone in the room, the panel granted the permit to the maverick company to continue its operation.

James, who had been a player in the stock market, said to Mike, "This is a real opportunity. This company trades on Wall Street. As soon as this news hits Wall Street tomorrow morning, the stock will triple."

"We should buy some of their stock," Mike said.

"You're right. Follow me," James said.

Outside the committee room, they called James's stockbroker and bought more stock than they could afford on margin. The next day, as predicted, the stock tripled and then tripled again.

"We need to sell because those rascals will be in trouble again," James predicted.

They agreed. James called his stockbroker, and the stock was sold at a tremendous profit. They put the money in GOB and Associates Incorporated to use for developing the business.

"What a windfall," James said. "Wow, lobbying has some real side benefits." They both laughed.

"This is legalized insider trading," Mike said.

"We now have almost one million in the GOB money market account," James said. "Can you believe it?"

Mike shook his head no and said he couldn't and then rolled his head and eyes back and upward. "I love this business. It's a dream job. Where could we make this much money with such little effort? Think about this. We could get our friends over at the environmental agency to jerk permits and put companies in the same situation as the one we just made all that money off of. Then we could repeat the same process and make millions."

"Right now we need to stick with lobbying. Such a scheme could backfire on us, and I am not certain what we did is completely legal," James said.

"Well, you're right, but we need to keep an eye out for a repeat situation." Sarcastically, Mike continued, "There's nothing wrong with making a million or two every now and then."

SECTION III

CLOSING AND STARTING AND REVEALING

CHAPTER 10

THANK GOODNESS IT'S OVER—WHAT'S NEXT

CLOSING OF THE FIRST SESSION

The closing night at the end of the session was interesting. Bills were being pushed all the way to midnight. At the end, crazy things were happening on the floor of the house and the senate. One senator went to the microphone and sang a song he made up about the governor. The entire senate joined in, and laughter roared. Mike and James were just enjoying watching the events on the way to the final gavel. If a lobbyist hoped to pass a last-minute bill on the last night, he was out of luck. This is why professional lobbyists made certain that time did not run out on their bills. The only things decided that night were major administrative bills, and those deals had already been cut.

The next day the capitol returned to the boring building it was before. Very few people were in the capitol, mostly state employees and some tourists. One door guard was playing solitaire, and another was sleeping on the job. There were few people in the coffee shop, and the café only served sandwiches. The work crews were servicing the elevators and refinishing some of the woodworking. The shoeshine stand was only open two days a week. Several independent lobbyists still met for coffee now and then.

At breakfast Mike related the legislature and lobbying to other parts of life. "There are two things that truly affect my thinking about life. The first is law school, and the second is our lobbying experience. Before lobbying I accepted most things at their face value. After this session of lobbying, I now see almost every issue in life as it relates to politics. The other morning I was looking at the cold and hot water in the bathroom sink. I wondered to myself who decided the cold should be on the right and the hot on the left. If the hot were on the right, the utility companies would make more money. Most people are right-handed, so it would be easier to reach the hot on the right side rather than reaching over for the left faucet. Did their lobbyist miss this opportunity? Then, I thought, everything is not political. Before lobbying I would never have thought of such. This business plays with your mind."

James laughed. "No, Mike, not ours, just yours. We have friends on all sides, in the middle and on both extremes of politics. I have antigun friends and friends who think everyone should be armed. I have racist friends and nonracist friends, pro-abortion and anti-abortion friends. This first session of lobbying taught me to look at both sides of political issues. It seems that in almost all political issues, something is happening behind the scenes that the general public is not aware of."

"You're definitely on target. Simple issues have complex and interwoven relationships behind the scenes that are unknown to the general public and the news reporters. The political columnists miss the underlying issues almost every time. They generally are no more informed than the public at large."

"Many of my friends select their friends based on their political beliefs," James said. "There are right-wingers who generally only have right-wing friends and left-wingers who generally only have left-wing friends. If they only knew what was going on behind the scenes, they would realize they were all getting screwed in one way or another. Then they would join together and go after the ones who were screwing them."

"You realize that we represent mostly business owners?" Mike pointed out.

"Yes."

"You know Colin, the lobbyist for the labor unions? We enjoyed talking to each other and had many good laughs over the different issues during the session. One day he told me he couldn't talk to me anymore during the legislative sessions because the head of the labor union said he was getting too close to a business lobbyist. I thought he was joking, but he wasn't. We only spoke in passing afterward. Can you believe that labor and business are so divided?"

"No, they are not that divided, except when it comes to an issue that is related to money, like who's going to receive the benefits and who's going to pay the most taxes creating division."

"It's all about money."

"Yes, but with maybe a sprinkling of sex and racism involved," James added. "When I was talking to the head of the statewide Homebuilders Association about sewage discharge in a lake—by the way, before I tell you the story, that ass is a guy you need to avoid. He doesn't want government to set standards for sewage treatment plants because he doesn't want government involved in home building whatsoever. I asked him how he could do that, because the standards are only to protect the health of citizens. He lit into me with a barrage of conservative points about government's involvement in business. I told him I agreed that government is too involved in business; however, there is a breaking point. For the next few days, he vocally condemned me to other lobbyists simply because I would consider letting government set standards for health reasons. He loudly called me a liberal just because I didn't want shit floating around in the water I drink. We lobbied for issues that kept government out of business during this session and issues that more than seventy percent of the public disagreed with. We, and the people we represent, are not so extreme that we won't listen to the other side. You agree?"

"Yes, I agree," Mike said.

"Of course, there are always two sides to every story," James said. "We represent concrete, and requiring high standards for sewage treatment plants would be 'good government' from the concrete companies' point of view. Concrete producers would provide the materials to build the damn plants."

"I guess we're just as guilty as the other lobbyists," Mike said.

WHAT DO WE DO NOW?

The next day James and Mike were talking about what was happening and what they had heard around the legislature recently. James said Bobby had told him that when the legislature was not in session, things slowed, but he still worked. Without thinking, Bobby had provided James a list, like a machine gun firing off bullets.

Bobby said, "These are the things I do between sessions." James made a list as Bobby spoke: "(1) Make daily contacts with bureaucrats and others who can influence legislation. (2) Visit legislators in their hometowns at their businesses or in their homes. (3) Recruit new clients and visit old clients throughout the state. (4) Entertain legislators who come to town for committee meetings. (5) Attend meetings of similar groups in other states. (6) Track legislation in other states related to clients. (7) Make an annual report to clients on legislation. (8) Visit each member of Congress, because federal legislation has an impact on state law. (9) Monitor, propose, and write regulations that will help my clients."

They divided these items and assigned responsibilities for each. After agreeing on the division, James and Mike made a schedule for completion of those items they considered important.

BE PREPARED, OR IT CAN GET NASTY

During their first session at a legislative hearing, James and Mike watched another lobbyist get massacred. Legislators questioned him intensely when they learned he did not know the answers to basic questions or much about the subject he had come before the committee to testify about. It was as if legislators resented any lobbyists telling them how to vote, and this was their opportunity to beat up on one of them.

"The lobbyist looked like a fool, Mike."

"Yes, and they were unmerciful," Mike replied. "They jumped on him like a pack of wild dogs that hadn't been able to find food for days and were fighting over one piece of meat."

"We never want to look like that," James said.

Donald had told the GOB that if a lobbyist wanted to stay in business, he had better be well prepared for committee hearings. These hearings were generally where a lobbyist won or lost, because when a bill got to the floor of the house and the senate, killing it became a difficult and time-consuming process. It kept echoing in their minds that two of their major clients had told them that if they lost, they were fired. They had already learned that if you can't kill a bill in committee, you can't expect to win on the floor. Never let a bill get to the floor unless you want it to get there. A lobbyist's job becomes much more difficult and time consuming at that level.

James told Mike, "It's also easier to fight a bill in the senate than in the house simply because there are fewer senators to convince to vote your way. Once a bill passes the senate, representatives are more likely to vote for it without a great deal of discussion."

Preparation was one of Mike and James's strengths. Mike came from a law school background. James had an undergraduate major in journalism and political science. He had studied political polling and dealt with statistics. He understood how to twist statistics in favor of his client. One of James's most outstanding skills was his ability to shine a light on the statistics he wanted to use to confuse the opposition and some legislators. He was also an outstanding public speaker. He could sell a person the Golden Gate Bridge if given enough time, especially if the person would allow James to show him why he needed it statistically. In the war room at the office, James could do amazing things with the numbers on the charts.

There are several ways to kill or pass a bill. One is the good-ole-boy backslapping, friendly approach. Many lobbyists were extremely talented at that. This meant knowing the legislator on such a personal basis that the lobbyist could put a hand on his shoulder and whisper in his ear, "My client needs your help on this bill, old buddy." The legislator may or may not be an "old buddy," but the lobbyist's personality could make him feel like he was. This system worked, but it took more time and a certain personality. With the Greenhouse, James and Mike certainly were developing a good-ole-boy relationship with legislators.

This good-ole-boy approach could easily be overcome by another lobbyist who came to a legislator with professional research and statistical analysis of the issue. This was especially true if the research showed the legislator why he was more likely to get reelected if he voted as the lobbyist needed him to vote. James and Mike learned that reelection was one of the highest priorities of almost all legislators. Research was certainly one of James and Mike's talents because of their education. By combining research and the GOB approach, they certainly were equipped to win. The concrete weight law bill would test those skills.

Another approach was the "feeding the monkeys" approach. This required almost a daily output of money to make contributions, so feeding the monkeys was an expensive way to handle legislation. Generally, only the Fortune 500s could afford this. In this case the personality of the lobbyist made no difference. James and Mike had consider-able expense money, but why waste it if it wasn't necessary? If they didn't spend it, they could keep it.

Was it easy to predict which approach would work? No, but one thing was predictable. The lobbyist who worked the committee before the hearing and knew how each legisla-tor was going to vote before the testimony was most likely going to be the winner, no matter which approach was used. James and Mike realized this and scheduled an appointment or had a "call to the side" conversation with every committee member before every bill they were interested in was heard in committee. On key bills that were of interest to one or more of their clients, they learned to start weeks ahead of time, visiting all the members on the committee where such bills would be heard. Some had been visited more than once. All had been invited to the Greenhouse.

There is another approach that is rarely used—that is, a call from the governor to the committee chairman, tell-ing him he wanted a bill passed or killed. The governor could make or break a bill any time. The governor was in an extremely powerful position. He handed out state contracts, which could be very lucrative to his friends and supporters. He could also direct money to different legislative districts for public projects that could make a local legislator look impor-tant and powerful. They call it "bringing home the bacon." It was easy for those legislators who brought home a load of bacon to get reelected. During the reelection campaign, the legislator could run ads showing the voters the projects he brought to the district. Those who failed to fetch the bacon were often defeated. Not only could the governor influence the passage of legislation, he could use an executive order and bypass the legislature. On major issues, the legislature might attempt to override his executive order.

A lobbyist who helped a governor get elected and had an open door to his office was a powerful person, especially one who helped the governor in the first primary. There was no limit to his fees. For example, one lobbyist who helped lead the elected governor's campaign told Mike and James he had one bill he had to show up for at the legislature. For the one-time appearance, he was paid $50,000. This is why some say, "If a lobbyist helps a governor get elected, he wins big, but if the lobbyist's candidate loses, good luck." The governor could also call clients and get the lobbyist fired. If that ever happened, the clients who loved their lobbyist so much would not walk across the street to talk to the lobbyist after the governor or his representative contacted them. Loyalty did not exist.

JUST FOR A PARKING SPACE

"We could write a book about the stories we hear," James said. "Did you know the head of the legislative staff had a fistfight with a man over a parking space in the garage?"

"No, really? Are you kidding?" Mike asked.

"I'm not kidding. He was charged with assault and battery and he got off. The district attorney dropped the charges. Maybe the DA believed that the beating was justified, because parking spaces are hard to come by around the capitol, especially during legislative sessions."

"No, he probably had some serious political connections," Mike said.

"Well, let's hope neither of us ever beats up anyone over a parking space," James replied.

John O. Murphy Ed.D.

THE KING'S ENGLISH

Either Mike or James was always sitting in the gallery of the legislature listening to legislators debate bills. One legislator in particular was very interesting to James. His name was Carl. He couldn't speak the King's English; he had his own local dialect. He couldn't match a subject and a verb. As James listened, he wondered how in the hell he could get elected. The lobbyist sitting next to James explained it to him.

"James, have you ever been to his district?"

"Yes."

"Did the people in the district look, sound, and act like Carl?"

"Yes."

"People vote for someone who looks like them, speaks like them, and acts like them. Carl is a perfect representative of his district, because he looks, speaks, and acts like the people near and around his hometown. You or I could never get elected in Carl's district." Then he pointed out, "Don't underestimate people like Carl. They're smart, just not sophisticated. Carl can swing more votes than you or I ever will."

At that moment James thought maybe Kimberly was right. She had told him he would make a perfect candidate for office because he fit the district in which he lived. *Maybe I could get elected to office*, James thought. He knew how to look good in front of a camera because he had worked at a television station for a few years. He spoke like, sounded like, and looked like the people of his district. The problem was James did not have the name recognition, a political base, or the money to fund the campaign.

HIRING JOSEPHINE

"We have so much money, we need to make sure we do everything right to keep it rolling in," Mike pointed out to James. "Josephine is a true asset. She has the personality and the devious mind that we need. Plus, she's female. I think we need to hire her full time."

"I agree. We both know she hates that law practice and would like to work with us."

"Nan is graduating next year, and we will be without office help," Mike said. "Let's call Josephine and offer her the position."

They called Josephine and asked her if she would meet them at the Capitol House Bar that afternoon. She agreed, and they met at five thirty. The usual crowd was in the bar. James walked around the bar in his politician mode and talked to each of the patrons, while Mike went straight to the table where Josephine was already sitting.

When James finally made it to the table to join them, Mike laughed and said to James, "I think if there were a baby in the bar, you would kiss it. You're a natural-born politician. Just watching you and not knowing who you are, a person would think you were the governor, a congressman, or someone like that." They all laughed.

After some small talk, Mike said to Josephine, "We have a proposal for you."

"You want me to screw both of you?" Josephine asked.

"No," Mike responded immediately. He laughed and added, "Do you ever think of anything except sex?"

"Occasionally."

"We would like you to come work for us full time," James said.

Without asking how much they would pay, Josephine said, "I'll take the job."

"You're taking the job without asking how much we will pay?"

"I know the Good Ole Boys will be good to me."

"We will pay you what you are making at the law firm, plus a bonus for any new clients you bring to the firm," James said.

"See, I told you the GOB would be good to me. I need to close out my job at the law firm, and that will take some time. Then I will come to work with you. I will make this happen as quickly as possible, but I must give lawyer Smith time to find my replacement. Does that work for you?"

"OK, we appreciate your concern for your present employer," James said. "Come as soon as you can."

"I hate to leave lawyer Smith because he's going to have to write his own petitions, answer discovery questions, write interrogatories, and work his ass off. His golf scores are not going to be good."

They all laughed, and James said, "Welcome aboard, Josephine."

She cheerfully replied, "I'll drink to that." They tapped their glasses together, and all took a swig.

SUPPORTING THE HORSES

Each year just after the session ended, a group of lobbyists sponsored "A Day at the Horse Races" at a track near the capital city. All the legislators were invited. They rode buses paid for by the lobbyists. The buses received a special escort by the state police on the highways and the police department in the city. The sirens and blue lights flashed all the way to the track. James and Mike volunteered to sponsor an early cocktail party. All legislators were invited for a morning coffee or cocktail.

Mike invited Mr. Jones, a wealthy man he wanted to represent as a lobbyist. He was very aware of city politics, but he had no concept of who represented the legislative districts statewide. Mike introduced him to senators and representatives from throughout the state. He shook their hands, smiled, and made small talk with them. After about thirty minutes, he took a seat on the sofa next to Mike. As they talked, he asked who and what about everyone while the two men observed the socialization taking place in the room.

Later Mr. Jones left to go to his business, but his remarks continued to spring forth in Mike's mind. He and Mike had continued to talk outside in the parking lot, and Mr. Jones had said, "That's a bunch of losers in there. They are just here to freeload off the lobbyists and the racetrack."

In general he was wrong, but about the group that attended the cocktail gathering that day, he was correct. Afterward Mike started to reexamine his view of the state legislators. Prior to that day, Mike had viewed each one of them with admiration because the legislators had been elected to represent the people from their home area. They had power Mike did not have.

For a few of them, their only success in life was being elected. They had not been successful in business, family life, or any other measure commonly associated with success. Some were elected because they spoke out and said the right thing at the right time and in the right place—nothing more than that and nothing less. On the positive side, some were elected because they had a wonderful vision for the state's future.

Mike's future opinions of legislators were reshaped by the combination of the wealthy client's assessment and the realization that the public elects people who looked and sounded like the voters in their district. Many people were not elected to the state legislature because they were successful or brilliant, although many of them were very successful and very bright. Mike then started to realize, but not surprisingly, that those who were successful in business outside the legislature were the ones who generally advanced to leadership at the capitol.

It also was interesting that some of the intelligent legislators concealed that fact with their country-boy mannerisms. In their cases, one certainly could not judge the book by its cover. Those who judged them that way made a big mistake. Since the day Mike said, "We could be lobbyists; let's start a lobbying firm," his entire opinion of the process and the legislature had changed. It was not just bullshitters bullshitting bullshitters. In most cases it was a deliberate, straightforward, and honest attempt to improve the state and districts from which they were elected.

SOMETHING FOR THE ENVIRONMENT

The gravel companies GOB represented were always having environmental problems. The companies they represented were multimillion-dollar operations. Most of them tried to follow the environmental laws, because it was less expensive than having to deal with environmental issues on the front page of the newspaper. The environmentalists were always watching gravel producers for several reasons. First, anytime the river flooded next to where they mined gravel, it washed out their holding ponds and muddied the river for fifty to one hundred miles or more. When that happened, environmentalists made certain the newspapers got a color picture of the river as a muddy body of water. Second and most important were the problems caused by the independent, small-time gravel operators who purchased a small dredging barge for a few thousand dollars. Without the money to build a holding pond, and because it was much less expensive to put the dredging barge in the middle of the river, they would start mining gravel from the river bottom. This muddied the river for miles, and every gravel producer on the river got blamed.

The newspapers were out to clean up the rivers. One gravel producer said, "During every session of the legislature, there would be a large color picture on the front page of the newspaper showing a gravel miner muddying the river by expelling wastewater back into the river." This was a public relations nightmare. Bills were introduced to completely stop gravel mining on the river. The bills were so extreme that the GOB killed them.

As a result of this attention given to gravel miners, James became personal friends with the head of the environmental agency. He was a big, overweight, friendly guy whom James enjoyed knowing. He had a private pilot's license, and the state had an airplane. He was trying to accumulate hours so he could get a more complex license, an instrument rating or something like that, so he could fly bigger airplanes. Routinely, James would get a phone call that would go like this:

"Hello, James."

"Dave, good to hear from you," James said. "I suppose we're going flying?"

"Yes, some of your gravel boys are in trouble. Let's go take a look."

"I'll meet you at the airport. What time?"

"Tomorrow morning at nine o'clock. Is that OK with you?"

"Yes, see you there."

The next morning promptly at nine o'clock, James met him at the local airport, and they boarded the state-owned airplane.

Often the airplane would be a land-sea model and could land on the water. James and Dave would fly the rivers from the state line all the way above the capital city and then return, landing at some restaurant on the water. Of course, James bought lunch.

During these flights there was always one target Dave wanted to point out to James. By target he meant a gravel producer who was muddying a river. Generally this meant that he had a complaint from a citizen or an environmental group such as the Sierra Club, or he just wanted to fly and used James and gravel as an excuse.

After the morning flight and lunch, Dave and James returned to the capital city airport. Upon arrival James did what was expected. He called the gravel producer and warned him that the inspectors were coming, and he needed to clean up his act immediately. The producers with any common sense immediately shut down their operation and retreated from their location near the river.

Now, everybody was happy. The Sierra Club or the citizen immediately saw the river clearing, and the gravel producer didn't make the headlines. Occasionally a belligerent gravel producer ignored James's phone call and warning. That was a real mistake, because the department inspectors would come down on the company like the US Army invading Europe during World War II. This relationship between the department head and James was good for the gravel producers who cooperated.

At a meeting with a very select group of the richest gravel producers, James suggested they become environmentalists and stop polluting the river. Before James could complete his suggestion, one producer said, "He doesn't have a damn beard, green hair, or a marijuana joint in his hand, and he is not wearing washed-out clothes." He was referring to James.

Then he said, "James, I thought you were on our side." James pointed out that because of his relationship with the head of the department, he could control the writing of the regulations, and all the small gravel operations would be put out of business because they could not afford to comply with the new requirements. Immediately everyone perked up, because if this happened, the large gravel producers would then dominate the market. James told them that the group in the room could write the regulations to require huge levees to prevent any runoff of muddy water into the river. These levees would cost millions of dollars to build, and a small gravel producer would not have the means or the resources to build such levees. This would eliminate competition and get rid of those producers who cause large companies costly problems. The large producers would become the environmentalists, the good guys. News reports would become positive rather than the constant bombardment of negative reports that had been a disastrous public relations nightmare. They could also require that the holding pond be built before the small producer could get a permit to operate.

The room got quiet. Then the largest producer in the room said, "James has a good idea. The small one-man barge operations in the middle of the rivers are costing all of us millions. They are here today and gone tomorrow, and we are left with the problems. They make it more difficult for us to make a profit." Then like a group of canaries, they all joined in, and the decision was made for the GOB to contact James's friend at the department and tell him the gravel producers would like to write regulations that would stop the muddying of the rivers. When James contacted Dave, he loved the idea.

For the next two months, James and a small group of large gravel producers wrote regulations. The department implemented the regulations, and the rivers ran clear. Was this good or bad? It made the environmentalists happy, but it eliminated competition in the gravel business. The big boys made a lot of money, and the mom-and-pop operations bit the dust. The American free enterprise system was no longer free. Mom-and-pops could not go into the gravel business because they could not afford the multimillion-dollar levees required by the new government regulations. The people James and Mike represented were happy, but the mom-and-pops could not afford a permit to operate.

The writing of the regulations was a top-secret operation. Only a few top officials in the department knew the gravel companies had written the regulations. Sometimes

James would say this was the best thing he had done as a lobbyist. Other times James regretted eliminating the mom-and-pops. Keep in mind there are always two sides to every issue. Many times it's difficult to determine which one is right. This was definitely good government for the big gravel producers but not so good for the mom-and-pops. It was good for the environment but bad for the free enterprise system.

CLOSER AND CLOSER

Kimberly and James spent all their free time together. They went to the movies, on picnics, to the beach, to plays, to music concerts, dancing at a cowboy bar, and shopping. They even went to the State Fair and rode the bumper cars and the Ferris wheel. They enjoyed each other's company and could not wait to see the other each day. When work separated them, they talked by phone all during the day. They went on day trips with friends and weekend trips to the beach.

A LITTLE THERAPY

During their first session, James and Mike had met the president of the State Occupational Therapy Association. She wanted to be on the state board that governs the licensing of therapists and medical doctors. She was at the legislature with a group of women and a few men who were trying to pass a bill to change the law to allow their person a seat on the board.

Later that year, after the group failed to pass the bill, the president of the organization called James and Mike. The amount offered to pay for the GOB's services was insignificant, but the work was interesting. If they passed the bill, the therapists would certainly hire Mike and James as their permanent lobbyist.

Again, the GOB learned to always keep in mind there may be something going on behind the scenes they don't know about. They also learned to always be nice to the losers when they were winning, because the roles could reverse. There is an old saying in politics: "Be nice to people on your way up, because those are the same people you will meet on the way down."

The State Medical Board, in addition to licensing the therapists, regulated their working conditions. The board determined the therapists' pay, training requirements, and working conditions, as well as what they could and could not do on the job. The occupational therapists had no representation on the board.

The therapist group hired James and Mike and asked them to pass a bill that would change the law and force the doctors to appoint one of the members of their profession to the board with the doctors of medicine. They claimed the doctors were in control of their profession and had little understanding of it. That was their only legislative interest. Mike got a representative to introduce a bill for the therapists to do just that. When the bill came up in committee, the lobbyist for the doctors was confident that James and Mike had no chance of changing the law. No other state had ever allowed such.

James asked the doctor's lobbyist/lawyer if they might work out a compromise, such as allowing one of the occupational therapists to be on the board without voting power. He rudely and arrogantly told James he had no interest in any compromise or even discussing it with him. What he didn't realize was that James had an ace in the hole. Later the lobbyist would wish he had discussed it with James.

James was good-looking and had a way with women. Several of the ladies in the group were attempting to get to know him better and would tell him things they would not tell Mike. Some of them were young, about his age, and had an interest in dating James. Two of the ladies had offered to buy James's lunch, and one had gone even further.

One of the ladies was sleeping with the married chairman of the committee, and she told James that the chairman breathed very hard during sex. Over pillow talk the chairman had told her he had gotten the governor to make some calls, and he would take care of the passage of the bill for her. When the votes were counted in committee, James won hands down. The doctors' lobbyist looked shocked. He could not believe the group of therapists had gotten the votes to override the doctors.

After the vote, the lobbyist came to James and said he would like to talk about the compromise James had suggested. James told him the group was no longer interested in talking about a compromise. The bill flew through the house of representatives and the senate. The occupational therapists now had a position on the medical board.

"Guess which occupational therapists the committee chairman got the governor to appoint to the doctor's board?" James asked Mike.

"The woman who was the mistress of the chairman!" Mike said, and laughed.

"You're correct, but it didn't take a genius to figure that out. Ain't politics interesting." He laughed and said, "Let's celebrate."

There was another lesson James and Mike learned with this group. They paid James and Mike the small fee and told them they were not interested in their services for the next session. In other words, they got a bargain. The GOB had spent hours working for them and had gotten them what they wanted, and then the therapists had fired the GOB.

"Never again will we do so much work for such little money," James said.

Mike scratched his head. "We could get a representative to introduce a bill next year to take them off the board."

"They would deserve what they got, but we need to just move on," James said.

"Yes, I was just joking, but I bet there are many lobbyists who would do just that."

CHAPTER 11

GOOD CLIENTS, GOOD TIMES

FUNERALS ARE GREAT, THE
MORE THE MERRIER

The funeral directors hired the GOB during the interim. James and Mike attended several of their meetings to learn more about the business. The funeral home owners were fun-loving and good-hearted people. They were never boring, and they were good businessmen.

Their meetings were not open to the public. As their lobbyists, the GOB got to attend the funeral directors' convention. This was an eye-popping event for both Mike and James. Neither had ever realized the suit coat a man is buried in did not have a back. The back was cut out to save material. The customer was not going to get out of the casket and walk around, so the back of the suit coat was not needed.

At the first convention the GOB attended, a salesman for a casket company was walking around the exhibit floor handing out small Styrofoam blocks. The Styrofoam blocks were carved out on each side to a different level. The salesman handed James the block, and James looked at it.

"What is this?" James asked.

"You're not a funeral director, are you?" he said.

James explained he was a lobbyist for the funeral directors, and the salesman immediately told James how the Styrofoam block was used.

"The block is placed under the corpse's head and rotated until the dead person or corpse looks natural and comfortable in the casket. At that point the corpse is injected with embalming fluid. Have you ever heard of the word *stiff*? The word *stiff* is used to describe the body after the embalming fluid is injected. The embalming fluid causes the body to become totally stiff. The Styrofoam block can then be removed and used on another customer. The customer's head would remain in the position it was in when the embalming fluid was injected. It would be stiff forever."

Then the salesman told James that of course a pillow was placed under the head to make the dead person appear to be sleeping. The salesperson laughed. "A stiff is really a stiff. If you push down on the head of a corpse in a casket, its feet will rise."

James and Mike learned a lot about death from the meetings they attended. Actually, they learned more than they wanted to know.

Several funeral directors were single. They told James it was difficult for a funeral director to get a date with a woman. When they told a lady what their job was, suddenly the lady had no time for them. They believed the term "funeral director" had a connotation of death and unhappiness. They pointed out that the profession had once been known as "undertakers or morticians." The name had been changed from undertakers to funeral directors to improve their image. The single guys, especially, thought it was time to make another name change. James told them he knew a state university professor who could bring together a research focus group and come up with a new name for the profession that would give funeral directors a new and better image. Then the GOB could pass a bill renaming the profession under state law

After the meeting, the professor and James had two martinis and laughed incessantly for an hour or more. They felt their pain and understood their desire to improve the imagery of the professional title. They realized that people were reluctant to have a positive image of anyone who dealt with death, no matter what the title. The study never materialized.

A smart lobbyist always hesitated to get involved in the creation and passage of a bill. As Mike and James had learned, it's much harder to pass a bill than to kill one. Such bills would take up hours and hours of their time. Unless a contract was drawn before the bill was introduced, there likely would not be any additional money paid for its passage. The funeral directors had two bills they wanted passed. Both bills were fascinating, but one of them they never completely understood. The client told them the bill was just a simple change in the administrative procedure. Nothing important. James and Mike worked the committee and had the votes to pass it, until the day of the committee hearing.

On that day five high officials of the Health Department appeared to testify against their bill. Mike knew one of them and called him outside the committee room before the hearing started to ask him what was going on. He said he knew all in their group were honest businesspeople. However, under this bill a death certificate could be issued in the town where the person died and another one issued in the place where he would be buried. Some way or another, this would allow insurance claims to be filed in two locations. Mike never quite understood the mechanism the official was referring to or if their group had dishonest intentions. He would rather think they were just trying to simplify the administration of death certificates. After the testimonies were heard, the committee deferred the bill. Deferral generally meant the bill was dead, but not killed, and the legislator offering the bill could bring it up later. The funeral directors saw the possible accusations that might be made and backed off. The bill died.

The next bill was absolutely funny. The funeral directors wanted to redefine the legal definition of the word *counseling*. It seems that one or two of them in other states had been sued for claiming they were counselors. One of them had counseled a widow all the way to her bedroom. The lawsuit claimed he had taken advantage of her when she was in a highly emotional state because of the loss of her husband. The discussion of the possibilities of a bill was extremely fascinating. Obviously more than one had done more counseling than needed. It was decided not to have a bill introduced because it would draw more attention to the problem. Rather, it was suggested that the term *counseling* not be used in the funeral director's job description.

"When it comes to the law, sometimes it's best to let sleeping dogs lie," Mike said. "Just one word can have an important impact on a company or individual."

"I agree," James said. "Sometimes that one word can cost the persons affected by the law a lot of money."

FLY, FLY AWAY

In September after the session ended, Kimberly announced to the legislative staff that she was going on vacation. That's all she told them. She never mentioned James or that she was going to Italy. She just said she would be back in two weeks. Kimberly certainly knew how to hold her cards close.

James and Kimberly had decided to go with two backpacks, as if they were kids again. In Rome they visited the open-air markets and tossed a coin into the Trevi Fountain. They shopped at the Campo de'Fiori, drank cappuccino, ate pasta, and visited the Pantheon and Colosseum. In the evening they drank wine at an outdoor restaurant that was Old World in every way. A sketch artist in the park drew their picture in crayon, and a palm reader read their palms. James dropped a euro or two in the collection cans of several street musicians. Neither had ever been happier, and it showed on their gleaming faces.

Kimberly fell more in love with James every minute. They learned they had complementary personalities. It was like a match made in heaven. But when Kimberly asked James if he loved her, his remark was, "Oh, I like you a lot," or something equally noncommittal. He would never use the word *love*. But Kimberly knew James had fallen in love with her. He was just afraid to admit it.

They traveled by train from Rome to Venice, where they rode in a gondola, visited art galleries, and stayed in a quiet hotel. They ate pizza made in a wood-burning oven in a small Venetian restaurant. They walked the narrow streets holding hands and fed the pigeons in the square. They watched the sunset over the water and drank wine while sitting by a large fountain filled with coins. Kimberly tossed in her coin and made a wish.

James knew he was in love with Kimberly, but he was concerned that he could be jumping into another relationship that would come to an undesirable end. He did not want to end up in another divorce. James believed marriage was forever and didn't want to be in a rebound marriage.

While sitting on a pier dangling their bare feet in the water, the conversation became more serious. Kimberly asked, "Is this a one-sided love?"

"No, it's not, Kimberly."

"Is that your way of telling me you love me?"

"You're the most wonderful person I've ever known. You're absolutely perfect. I would marry you today, right now, but I don't want to jump into a marriage that won't work out in the end. The next person I marry, I plan to have children and grandchildren and grow old with that person."

"When we marry, that is the way it will be."

"How can you be so sure?"

"Believe me, I know," Kimberly said.

That night they had dinner at an old, small, candlelit European restaurant. It looked a lot like the old restaurant in James's neighborhood back home that Kimberly enjoyed so much.

"Hello! Just married?" the waiter asked.

"Why would you think that?" Kimberly asked.

"Because you look like you're just married and belong together. You are both beautiful people who look like you are in love."

"No, we're not just married, but I'm going to marry him when he gets the courage to ask me, and he will. I just have to give him more time."

The three laughed, and James ordered a bottle of Chardonnay.

After dinner they walked to the pier where they had hung their feet in the water earlier that day. The night air was wonderful. The full moon was beautiful over the water.

"The moon diamonds are beautiful," James said.

While they had their arms around each other, James said, "Kimberly, I accept your proposal for marriage."

"Wonderful," she said, and she kissed him intently.

"I'm not a rich man, but I have an engagement ring for you. It's not impressive, but it's the best I can do today." James had a little plastic ring like one you would get out of a box of Cracker Jack. He placed it on her left-hand ring finger and said, "Kimberly, I love you. Will you marry me?"

"Yes, yes. I have waited years for someone like you. I knew the first night we were I was going to be with you for the rest of my life. This is the most beautiful ring I have ever seen. I suppose we're now engaged?"

"Yes. You did accept, didn't you?"

With great joy in her voice, she said, "Yes, I accept. I love you, I love you, I love you, James."

Kimberly was the happiest woman in Venice.

"I will get you a better ring when we return to the States," James said.

Kimberly quickly said, "No, this is all I want. There is no better ring than this. I will wear it every day until our wedding day and keep it the rest of my life." She laughed and said,

"How many girls do you know who have a ring like this?" They both laughed and hugged.

Kimberly pushed him on his back on the pier, and they lay side by side listening to the water movement and looking at the moon for hours. They talked about their future life together, the wedding, and children.

As they got up to leave, James said in an alarming voice, "Kimberly, have you noticed that man who seems to be following us? I've seen him somewhere before. I think I saw him near my apartment."

Kimberly casually said, "Oh, that's Jack."

In a startled voice, James said, "Jack? You know him?"

"Yes, he follows me everywhere."

"Is he crazy?"

"No, he's my security guard. Jack makes sure we are not kidnapped."

"Wait a minute, you need a security guard?"

"Yes, James. Jack is one of the disadvantages of being wealthy."

"Wealthy? What do you mean? You have a very nice condo, but that doesn't mean you're rich."

"There's more you don't know about, James. I hope my family's wealth does not scare you away. I didn't tell you because I had to be certain you wanted me for myself and not for my family."

James thought for a minute and then said, "You're kidding."

"We could give it all up. I will if you want me to."

"Why would you want to marry a guy like me?"

"Because I love you. It's not about wealth."

"I don't know about all this!"

"You can't back out now, just because I have a few more toys than the other girls. You see this little plastic ring on my finger? It's a lifetime commitment, and I am never letting you go. We are going to grow old together."

She pushed a button on an alert pad in her purse, and within seconds Jack was standing beside them.

"May I help you, Miss Kimberly?"

"Jack, I want you to meet James, my fiancé."

"Well, I suppose congratulations are in order."

Jack shook James's hand, and James asked, "Haven't I seen you around before?"

"I assume Kimberly has told you the nature of our relationship. I try to remain discreet."

"You've done a good job of doing that."

"Thank you, sir," Jack said. "I will move on now, Miss Kimberly, if that's OK?"

"Certainly, Jack."

The next morning Kimberly asked James if he would mind taking a detour on the way home.

"A detour, what do you mean?"

"I would like to go through Paris. We have a home there that you've never seen. Matter of fact, I haven't seen it in two years."

The next day Jack had their airline tickets changed to go to Paris. In Paris Kimberly had a wonderful townhouse overlooking a beautiful park.

They spent four days exploring Paris. Kimberly showed James the sights of Paris and explained the history of each one. She took him to meet some of her Paris friends she hadn't seen in a long time. They were an eclectic group of fun-loving, nice people. They all welcomed James with open arms. Kimberly had spent several summers in Paris and had learned to speak French fluently.

James asked Kimberly why she worked in state government.

"Because I like good, real people, and many of them are very good people. They are struggling to make their house payments and car notes and pay for their children's education. They are just good, basic people. The politics of the place are fascinating, and I wanted to learn more about the inner workings of the process. I never tell any of them about any of this because I want them to know me as they see me, not as some spoiled, rich girl. When people know about your wealth, they look at you differently. You never know if they are friendly toward you because of your wealth or because they like you as a person."

On their return flight to the States, they couldn't keep their hands off each other. But it was back to work and back to the real world. Upon returning to his office, James was welcomed by Mike, Josephine, and Nan. They asked him how the trip was and so on, and he said it was wonderful. At her office Kimberly was told she looked refreshed and happy. There was something different about her smile. One of the legislative staffers noticed the plastic ring on her finger and asked what it was.

Kimberly smiled, laughed, and answered, "Oh, it's a little ring out of one of those Cracker Jack boxes. A friend gave it to me."

The staffer said, "And you are wearing it on your ring finger?"

"Yeah," Kimberly said. "That was the only finger it would fit."

The staffer laughed and said, "Well, I hope you won't marry some guy who would give you something like that."

"Oh, you can't judge a book by its cover or a giver by the gift." Kimberly did not mention her engagement because she knew her fellow workers would read about it on the society page.

UNDERSTANDING THE BUREAUCRAT

The state fire marshal called the GOB office and made an appointment to talk to James about funeral home construction. He told him he was going to propose legislation to regulate the construction of funeral homes. He specifically wanted to talk about the construction of cremation rooms. It seems that in another state a four-hundred-pound man had been cremated and the heat produced so much fat and grease that it somehow overflowed. The burning grease and fat caused the cremation room to catch fire. This resulted in burning down the entire funeral home.

James called the owner of a large chain of funeral homes and asked if he had an architect who could sit in on the meetings with the fire marshal. He did; the architect's name was Tom. The owner sent him to the meeting. He told the state fire marshal he had been working for funeral homes most of his life and had never seen a fire caused by the cremation process. "Laws and regulations were unnecessary," Tom said.

"A bill is going to be introduced in the next year or two, and I hope to have the support of funeral home owners," the fire marshal said.

"We would rather police ourselves," the architect said.

Seeing that the meeting was going nowhere and that they disagreed on the way to prevent fires, James interrupted the meeting and said, "Let us study the issue and get back to you."

"OK, that will be fine," the fire marshal said. "I look forward to hearing from you."

The architect and James bid the marshal good-bye.

"We will do nothing and likely we will never hear from that bureaucrat again," James said. "He probably just needed something to do today." James continued, "He will go back to his office and write a report about our meeting that will go into a file, and it will never be read again. Of course he will collect his travel expenses for driving to the meeting. I'm surprised he didn't hang around for a free lunch."

"I've never gotten to design an entire facility," Tom said. "I wish the fire in the other state had been in one of our buildings so I could have had the opportunity to build a funeral home from the ground up." They both laughed.

As James had predicted, they never heard from the bureaucrat again.

FOOTBALL

Mike told James they needed some perks of some kind to hand out to legislators and clients, such as football tickets. He pointed out that he got calls routinely asking for football and basketball tickets. James told Mike he had met the chancellor of the university and the football coach during one of the legislative hearings and had coffee with them.

"I'll call and see if they can get us some good tickets," James said.

"No, James, make an appointment and go talk to them. As my father told me, when something is important, look a man in the eye, and these tickets are important."

"I'm on it. I'll make an appointment and drive over to the university to talk to one of them about tickets. This trip could be interesting."

"Pay whatever they ask. We need the tickets."

James called Kimberly and told her what he was doing. He asked her if she would like to ride with him, but she was too busy. She added, "Wave your magic wand."

"What is this magic wand you're always talking about?"

"It's just a joke."

"Maybe you can explain the joke to me someday," James replied.

Kimberly laughed and said, "You'll figure it out someday. You're a smart boy."

The visit to the university was more eye-opening than James had expected. First he went to the coach's office. The coach told James the chancellor wanted to meet him, so they walked across campus to the chancellor's office. The chancellor and the coach talked to James about the importance of funding the university. They pointed out to him that the buildings on the campus were deteriorating because of the lack of maintenance. They showed him how the concrete people could make thousands of dollars providing concrete, and his building materials clients could provide materials for the maintenance, repair, and rebuilding, if the legislature did not delete their maintenance requests from the budget.

They wanted to know if James would help them. He knew that to prepare for the next session, budget hearings would be conducted during the interim. James, not expecting this conversation, did not know what to say. He told them he would look into it.

"James, if you help us with this, we will provide you with several season tickets. We have heard about your success and the Greenhouse," the coach said.

"Would you let us know next week, if possible? The staff is already assigning season tickets," the chancellor added.

"I will let you know this afternoon after I meet with my partner. I feel certain he will agree, but first I need to pass it by him," James replied.

James called Kimberly from the university and told her about the conversation.

Kimberly's mother and father had donated millions to the university. A phone call to the chancellor from Kimberly before James arrived had brought about this opportunity for the GOB, but Kimberly was not revealing this to James. Kimberly thought James did not need to know everything.

When James returned to the office, he told Mike about the meeting.

"That's interesting, James. I never thought of such an offspring relationship. We don't have much to do at this time, so we could talk to some of the committee members here at the Greenhouse and invite the chancellor and the coach for lunch so they can make their pitch in this informal atmosphere."

"It looks like a win-win situation for us. We swing a few votes and get some amazing tickets to provide to potential and current clients."

"You call them back, James, and tell them we're working on it, and we would like to be a part of their team."

"OK, what a deal!"

"It's sort of funny," Mike said. "Neither of us cares that much about football, and fans who are crazy about it can't get tickets."

The next day James received several sets of season tickets by express mail. Mike strategized. "We need to be cautious about who knows we have these tickets. We will have legislators competing for them to give to their constituents, and they could put us on the spot about which one gets the tickets."

"OK, we will not tell anyone that we have these seats on the fifty-yard line. We will just tell legislators that we might be able to find some for them. If they are voting with us, we will give them a ticket to one or two games. If they're not with us, we will tell them we can't get any tickets."

"You know, James, these tickets are more important than the private airplanes. Together they are a home run. Brown Timber may want to help."

The university budget hearing came up before they had the opportunity to set up the meeting at the Greenhouse as they had planned. On the day the state university budget items were being heard in committee, James and Mike were present. They were following through on their promise to the chancellor and the coach for the football tickets. They called the chancellor aside and asked him who was voting for and against them.

"We're going to lose this today because the following are against us," the chancellor said. He gave James their names.

"Let us talk to some of them," James said.

James talked to some of them while Mike talked to others. Then they called the chancellor aside.

"This is the deal," James said. "Senator Abraham wants his daughter accepted into law school."

"How did she do on the entrance exams?" the chancellor asked.

"She was just one point under the required test score. She has a three-point-nine-seven undergraduate GPA."

"Tell the senator she will be accepted. I will talk to the dean tomorrow, and it will happen."

"Senator Macpherson wants to handle some of the university's legal affairs in his law office," Mike said.

"Tell him we will send him some business," the chancellor said.

The bill was heard and passed out of the Budget Committee, only because James and Mike were able to convince the chancellor to provide a few perks for the legislators. When the legislature convened, the bill quickly passed the house and senate without any discussion. The chancellor was very happy. He only had to provide two more law school entrants, one medical school enrollment, one part-time law school teaching assignment for one representative, and the rental two small buildings that the university did not need. There was unused space on the campus, and now the university had to rent from contributors and constituents of a few legislators just to get the money to maintain and repair the buildings on campus. James and Mike had been instrumental in cutting all the deals.

Fortunately, the organizations that accredited the university allowed a 5 percent deviation from admissions requirements, and that factor helped in the negotiations. Legislators were able to get family members and constituents into medical and law school because of this. The admissions deviation was a powerful political tool.

"I thought all admissions to law school were based on a formula, and the same for medical school," James said to Mike. "I never imagined that a person teaching in a university got his job because of some maintenance budget dealings in the state legislature."

"Yes, James, I never cease to be amazed."

"If the taxpayers knew the whole story, they would quit paying taxes."

At a breakfast staff meeting one morning, James told Mike about a conversation with Mr. Dwight of Brown Timber.

"I told Mr. Dwight about the ticket deal with the state university and how we had managed to get several tickets to their football games for helping improve the university budget. Mr. Dwight said that was a win-win deal for us. He said some of the legislators would do almost anything for such tickets. And if we wanted to use one or two of Brown Timber's airplanes to fly the motherfuckers, it was no problem. He also said to call him if we needed any help with the state university's budget problems, and he would get right on it," James said.

"Good, James, we will take him up on his offer."

SECTION IV

ROUND TWO

CHAPTER 12

HERE WE GO AGAIN

INTRODUCTION TO SECOND SESSION

The next year during the second session, the same bills that came up during the first session were introduced again. James and Mike employed the same methods to kill the lumber tax, truck weight laws, and other bills that they used in the first session. The Good Ole Boys and Associates had learned the routine and had become recognized as significant players in the state political process.

They learned that the gutter language they had used in their previous employment would not play well in the state legislature. Associating with powerful political figures had become a daily event. They knew who pulled whose strings and how to twist an arm.

At their breakfast meeting Mike said, "Have you seen that group of fools who were picketing at the state capitol yesterday?"

"Yes, they don't really think that picketing has an impact on the voting, do they? Most of the time, they are ignored," James said.

"I just learned something we can't ignore. Representing concrete can be very dangerous," Mike said.

"Dangerous? What do you mean, Michael?"

"Price-fixing," Mike replied.

"What do you mean, price-fixing?" James asked.

"Price-fixing is when competing businesspeople get together and set a price for their product, which they will all then charge the customer. Just suggesting that everyone charge the same price or increase the price of a product in a meeting is a violation of the federal antitrust laws. Everyone in the group could go to jail, especially if the prices go up the next day. If you hear a person make the suggestion to set prices and you don't report what you heard to the US attorney, you could be charged with a felony. If you report it, then you become a witness against your client, and all your other clients will fire you. It's a catch-22 situation," Mike explained.

"You're damn right! It sounds like it," James said. "Where did you hear this?"

"From a lawyer at a cocktail party Catherine and I attended last weekend. Several years ago he represented a concrete producer and a former executive director of the Concrete Association who had a price-fixing scheme," Mike said.

"Did his clients go to jail?" James asked.

"Yes, they did," Mike said. "The lawyer said both served five years in a federal penitentiary. The executive director/lobbyist was instructed by a concrete producer to go from one concrete dealer to another statewide, telling them to go up on the price of concrete, and several of them did. One of the men they visited turned them over to the US attorney."

"Hell, how do we protect ourselves?" James asked. "One of those fools might just step up in a meeting and say let's all increase the price of concrete by thirty dollars per yard, and the other idiots do it. No wonder Mr. Gonzales changed his mind and decided to hire us. He couldn't get any other fools to represent them."

"I hope you're wrong, but you could be right." Mike said. "The antitrust law issue exists in all businesses, but concrete seems to be involved more than other industries. One thing's for certain. We need to keep our mouths shut and avoid any gatherings of concrete producers when possible. Attend meetings when asked to report on legislation and get our asses out of there as quickly as possible. I'm damn glad we're just the lobbyist and not involved in meetings and having to keep notes or anything like that. Fuck, no wonder so many concrete producers show up at the meetings with their lawyers. I'm going to break out my old lawbooks and read about the antitrust laws."

"That's a good idea," Mike.

Later, Kimberly suggested they get a lawyer to talk to them about this issue. She said they should contact the Smith, Smith, and Smith law firm. They specialized in antitrust violations.

"OK, I will set up a meeting as quickly as possible," James said.

"I forgot to mention that the lawyer said that in the southern part of the state, an employee of a concrete company was caught wearing a wire just a few months ago. The good news is he was not employed by any of the companies we represent," Mike said.

"How did they catch him?"

"The owner got suspicious. He purchased each employee a shirt with the company logo on it and asked each one to try it on in front of him and other employees in his office. The employee refused to do so; they tore his shirt off and exposed the wire."

"What happened to the employee?" James asked.

"I don't know. He's probably missing. Maybe he's buried under a concrete slab."

"What the hell; the prerequisite to progress is risk. No risk taken means no progress is made in business. Plus, there are a multitude of lobbyists who would love to represent the concrete people if we quit. All business has risk. We just need to proceed with caution," James said.

They both laughed and moved on to another subject.

CAN'T LOSE THIS ONE

It seemed that every lobbyist had a bill or bills that identified him—in other words, a bill that tested a lobbyist's political clout and one he became known for. One of the GOB's was a bill that required a tarpaulin on sand and gravel trucks. This was certainly an interesting issue. A poll conducted by one legislator revealed that more than 90 percent of the people in the state wanted to see tarps over the loads of sand and gravel trucks. James and Mike agreed with the public; loaded trucks needed their loads covered, especially sand and gravel trucks. Rocks falling off the trucks broke windshields, and some said the rocks were a serious road hazard.

A senator introduced a bill to require tarps on all sand and gravel trucks. The gravel producers wanted it killed. Why would they want that? The answer was simple. The gravel industry did not want to spend the money and time to cover the sand and gravel trucks. Furthermore, they did not want government involved in their business in any way. Defeating this bill would send a message to legislators and bureaucrats not to mess with the gravel industry. Killing it made a legislator think twice before introducing a bill opposed by the gravel industry.

The next obvious question was, how would the GOB kill such a popular bill when more than 90 percent of the public was in favor of its passage? It wasn't easy. It was a real challenge.

"If we lose this bill, it will make us appear weak as lobbyists," Mike said. "Killing it will give us serious recognition, because no one believes such a good government bill could be killed. If killed, it will show that the sand and gravel industry and the GOB are a political force to be reckoned with. The legislature is like the bully in the schoolyard. The industry must stand up to them, or they will run over the industry."

The procedure James and Mike used to kill the tarp bill was interesting. Beating public opinion is not easy especially when such a large percentage of the public wanted tarps to be placed on sand and gravel trucks.

First, James and Mike talked to leaders in the industry, who helped them develop talking points to rally sand and gravel producers statewide. The talking points would not provide reasons the bill should be passed, only reasons to kill it. Talking points were as follows:

1. The bill would allow big government to interfere unnecessarily in the sand and gravel business.
2. If they, referring to the bureaucrats and legislators, won this one, there would be more and more

regulations. Sand and gravel producers couldn't let them get their foot in the door.

3. Rocks come from the shoulder of the roads, not from the gravel trucks. Cars were throwing the rocks, not the gravel trucks.

4. The Department of Transportation failed to cover the shoulders of the road with asphalt or concrete. Therefore, the department was causing the problem because it failed to build an appropriate highway. The rocks were coming from the shoulders, not the trucks.

5. There were no rocks on a gravel truck to fall and break a windshield. When the trucks leave the gravel pits, the rocks fall off when they drive on the unpaved roads leading out of the pits. Most legislators had never seen a gravel pit and didn't know whether this was true or not. At some gravel pits it was true, and at others it was not.

6. Mike and the CPA developed a cost estimate for the gravel industry showing the large impact on the cost of construction. They calculated the cost of the tarp and the time required to pull the tarp over the load and tie it down. They claimed a gravel truck made six loads a day. Since it took a man twenty minutes to pull the tarp and tie it down, the cost to the industry became astronomical. Six loads times twenty minutes equaled 120 minutes per day. This totaled two hours per day in labor costs. Multiply this by the number of gravel trucks a company owned—some owned twenty to forty gravel trucks—and one could see why the gravel industry became interested in this bill.

Truthfully, there are several gaping loopholes in this argument. Legislators were busy and didn't take the time to calculate or challenge the cost. It was not the gravel industry's responsibility to provide the opposition with their arguments.

7. Next, gravel producers were told to point out to companies or industries that buy gravel that their cost would increase. Then James and Mike would have another large group helping to kill the bill.

8. Point out that gravel was mined in only two sections of the state. Therefore the problem existed only on two less-traveled highways. Why punish an entire state for a local problem?

9. Passing a tarp bill in most sections of the state would not help a representative or senator get reelected. It would make a legislator appear to be an enemy of small business. So why should a legislator get involved in the issue? Legislators from those parts of the state where gravel mining took place were certainly not stupid enough to take on a major employer like the gravel industry.

Once these points were distributed to sand and gravel businesses, calls to legislators and other businesses started immediately. The grassroots network was working to kill the bill; however, there was not enough time to kill it in committee. Senator Jackson told the boys not to worry; he would take care of it on the senate floor.

An unexpected development was the newspaper's front-page story concerning the department's failure to pave the shoulders. The department leaders were unhappy. James and Mike had made the department the bad guys, and it was reported in the newspaper for the whole world to read. The sand and gravel industry was no longer the focus of attention.

"I'll bet you a thousand dollars the department staff will never sponsor a tarp bill again," James said. "It was almost funny seeing and hearing the department officials trying to defend themselves. In reality they had really done nothing wrong. The officials are certainly unhappy with the gravel industry, but they were not a friend to the industry anyway. Most of the time, they were against the industry. So what if they are a little angry?"

The bill passed out of the senate committee and got to the senate floor. Old Senator Jackson from the Capitol House Bar introduced an amendment that would kill it. The amendment introduced required a tarp on chicken trucks, farm trucks, vegetable trucks, livestock trucks, and any other truck that hauled a product in the open air. One legislator, who was a friend of the gravel industry, wailed like a preacher on the microphone, proclaiming that chicken feathers were dangerous.

"Gentlemen, we must stop allowing these chicken trucks to scatter feathers all over the state's highways," he said. This legislator, from a rural area of the state, made one of the funniest presentations ever made in the state legislature. He spoke at the microphone for more than fifteen minutes about the danger of feathers on the road. Legislators were laughing uncontrollably.

Another rural legislator took the microphone and spoke about the grain trucks. He claimed that grain falling off the trucks on the highway was dangerous, and the trucks should be covered. He even went so far as to say that grain farmers were tracking mud onto the highway. He added that they should be required to wash each truck that entered the highway from the grain field. At this point the State Farmers Association joined in to help kill the amendments and the bill.

Another legislator whose brother was in the gravel business took the microphone and requested that trucks transporting pigs be included in the law. The reason he gave was the odor was so overwhelming he could not roll down his car windows when following a truck loaded with pigs.

The list of industries included in the amendment was long and ridiculous. The debate became so funny that even the most serious-minded legislators had to laugh. The amendment motivated the grain producers, ranchers, pork producers, chicken farmers, and many others to want the bill killed. The bill died a sudden death.

"It's amazing how a lobbyist can bring pressure to bear on a legislator," James said.

CONNECTIONS, CONNECTIONS

"I got another damn speeding ticket," Mike complained.

"Talk to the sheriff's lobbyist," James said. "You know him. His name's Linn. He will take care of it, and if he can't, he will talk to Jerry, the District Attorney Association lobbyist. One or the other will take care of it for you, or they will tell you who will."

"That's one of the many advantages of this business," Mike said. "We know people who can take care of almost anything, and they will do it for us because they never know when they will need our support. If one of them can't take care of it, I'll talk to one of the governor's bodyguards. They are connected to the state police."

"What a great system for those of us in it. I never imagined we could develop so many connections." James laughed and said, "I love this job."

WE TRIED TO TELL YOU

Later, a state representative took another shot at passing the tarp bill in a future session. The GOB approached him and offered to take him to lunch to discuss the bill. They pointed out that the gravel industry might consider some concessions. They liked him and did not want him to get a black eye from a bill they knew had no chance of passing. He told James and Mike no thanks. He was going to pass the bill as written, and there would be no compromise. The GOB had worked the committee and knew the bill was dead. Before the hearing they suggested he not bring it to a vote, because they knew he was going to lose.

"I have polled my district and found that almost all the voters are in favor of tarps on gravel trucks," the representative said. He showed the GOB a copy of the polling he had done and said he was going to present it to the committee. "There's no way I can lose."

He proposed his legislation and did an excellent job. During his presentation he gained the support of one of the representatives, a legislator named Ted, who said, "A gravel truck broke my freaking windshield on the way to the legislature this morning, and I was in my brand-new Mercedes-Benz."

The chairman of the committee, who was on the gravel business side, said, "Your brand-new Mercedes-Benz?"

"How many committee members have a brand-new Mercedes-Benz?" the chairman asked. No other committee members raised their hand. Instead, laughter broke out. The chairman kept attacking the representative's Mercedes-Benz. Rather than hearing about the bill, it became a time to tell jokes about the rich who own Mercedes-Benzes. James and Mike sat in amazement. The chairman was doing the dirty work for them.

The chairman then asked, "Would you gentlemen"—referring to James and Mike—"buy Representative Ted a new windshield for his Mercedes-Benz?"

"Yes," James and Mike said.

The chairman said, "Now, that solves the problem. No one wants to see this bill passed."

The vote was taken, and James and Mike won by a large majority. The representative who had introduced the bill looked shocked. After regaining his composure, he came to James and Mike outside the committee room and said, "I will take you men up on that lunch now."

"We have no interest in lunch," Mike said. "You lost." Later, they had lunch with him and laughed about the entire procedure.

He told the GOB they taught him to listen when a lobbyist speaks. "I can't believe you were able to kill such good legislation." The GOB agreed.

James and Mike wondered why the insurance companies didn't get involved in the tarp bill. Insurance companies were paying for the broken windshields. The GOB figured the insurance companies just didn't realize what was happening. Their lobbyist had overlooked it. James and Mike certainly didn't want to bring it to their attention because they were powerful, and it would be difficult to beat them. Let the sleeping dog lie.

However, James couldn't stand it any longer, so after the tarp bill was dead, he approached one of the insurance lobbyists and asked why they were not supportive of such a bill.

"Do you think we are stupid?" the insurance lobbyist said. "Windshield breakage by gravel trucks costs us about five million per year. We sell forty million more in insurance because people are concerned about a gravel truck breaking their windshield. It's a profit center for us." He laughed and said, "James, you and Mike keep up the good work."

"Damn, it's so easy to kill a tarp bill," James said. "I need a wolf at the door. Please come and support the tarp bill next session."

"Sorry, we can't help you," the insurance lobbyist responded.

Of course James was joking, because the last thing he needed was opposition from the insurance companies. They were bigger than the GOB, and if they took an active role in opposition to a tarp bill, the Good Ole Boys would likely lose.

A GOOD IDEA FOR GOOD OLE LOBBYIST

Bobby walked up to the table and said. "Hey guys, I can't stop and talk because I am running late, but I want to throw out an idea for all of you to think about before I run down the hall to a committee hearing." Bobby quickly suggested a change in the regulation of lobbyists. "One of us should get a legislator to add an amendment late one night to require all want-to-be lobbyists to take a course in lobbying ethics, pass a test, and pay higher fees. This would eliminate most of the volunteers and provide a new source of clients for us. We could grandfather us in and not have to take a course or test by simply adding a statement that exempts those who have been registered and testified before a committee as least one time before the law was signed by the governor. Most of the volunteers have never testified and would be eliminated. We could also increase the registration fees. I can't talk now, but all of us should think about it. We will talk later."

As Bobby left for the committee hearing, Paul said, "That is not a bad idea."

Donald agreed and said, "We need to have a meeting after we all have had time to ponder the idea. We need to think about who would administer the test and offer the course. There are some in the administration who would like to eliminate all of us."

"I'll get Bobby to call a meeting," Paul said.

IT'S DIFFICULT BEING A GOOD CITIZEN

Realizing that the tarpaulin bill was giving the gravel industry a black eye, the owners of the gravel companies asked the GOB to get a legislator friendly to the gravel industry to file a bill with reasonable requirements to tarp sand and gravel trucks. James got a legislative staffer in Kimberly's office to draft the bill. The gravel companies reviewed it and agreed to the stipulations. It included such things as not requiring a tarp if the delivery was less than thirty miles. Modest fines were included. James thought that battling this bill was over. How wrong he was. When the bill came up on the floor, several amendments were introduced. One required washing the truck just before it entered the highway from the gravel pit. Another required that each truck be driven over a cattle guard to shake off loose rocks before it entered the highway. This meant that every pit owner would have to build a cattle guard. One wanted a state inspector to approve each truck as acceptable before it could get on the highway. The list continued and was so ridiculous that James could not believe what happened to their effort to compromise. The bill passed out of the house of representatives, but it was killed in the senate committee.

"I've learned never to compromise when I'm winning. Welcome to the real world of politics. It ain't always pretty," James said. "It's like a famous Prussian statesman said, 'Laws are like sausages; it is better not to see them being made.' I think his name was Bismarck, and he lived during the eighteenth century."

FRIENDS, ENEMIES, AND POLITICOS

Sometimes lobbyists had to walk a narrow line. Legislators took some things very personally. One extremely large, fat, and loudmouth legislator pretended to be a good friend to James and Mike. He did that because they represented a grassroots group that controlled a large vote in his district. He didn't like Mike and Mike knew it. But that was OK because he had to vote the way the GOB wanted or they could report his vote against the group they represented, and that would not go over well in his district.

Donald told the GOB that as independent lobbyists they should report a legislator's vote against the people in his district only as a last resort. It was like throwing a rock at the legislator and hitting him on the head. He was certainly going to pick up that rock and throw it back at you. He would likely become a lifetime enemy. An independent lobbyist could not afford many of these. The large business or labor groups could afford to throw rocks, but the independent lobbyist could not. The large groups had more money and power than the individual legislator. They could put up large sums of money for a candidate to run against him. Donald pointed out to James and Mike that they and other independent lobbyists didn't have the resources to take on a legislator. All of them just had to be nice guys.

However, Mike had reported big fat Bill's votes to some of his constituents. Fat Bill was out to get Mike, but he died suddenly one afternoon of a massive heart attack during the session on the floor of the house. Big fat Bill was gone forever. Mike celebrated his passing by buying everyone coffee at Donald's table.

GOOD PEOPLE JUST TRYING TO HELP

The governor made James a colonel on his staff. He was given a large certificate with his name on it, proclaiming him a colonel. The certificate looked and sounded important, but both Mike and James knew the certificate was a worthless piece of shit.

"I must tell you how a man in the western part of the state failed to realize the political power he had," Mike said. "While I was visiting with the man, he told me how he had painted one thousand signs on four-by-eight sheets of plywood, delivered them statewide, and installed them on the side of the road for a candidate for governor.

"He was proud of the fact that he was one of the very first men in the state to do anything to help this candidate for governor. This man used his personal vehicle, purchased the gas, and spent weeks delivering and installing the signs on the side of the road, in fields, and in corner lots. As he told the story, I could remember seeing those early signs on the side of the road. I was very impressed by the professional appearance of them and how they portrayed such a positive image of the candidate."

James asked Mike if the governor remembered the man after he was elected, knowing that in the political arena, no one in politics did something like this for nothing.

Mike responded with a rapid and direct yes.

During Mike's visit, the man quickly and proudly pointed to the wall to show him the certificate signed by the governor proclaiming him a colonel. The sign maker said that the governor called him after the election and asked what he wanted, and he told him he wanted to be a colonel on his staff. To him such a designation was important.

"This man could have gotten almost anything he wanted," Mike said. "He didn't realize that certificate was just a worthless piece of paper. He also didn't realize that governors don't call people and ask what they want unless they are extremely important to him. People call the governor and beg to get what they want. He could've been a high official in government or had a contract to perform a service for the state that could have paid millions."

"I can't believe what I just heard," James said, shaking his head. "This man was just a good citizen trying to help someone he believed in and he thought would help the state. As lobbyists we lose the concept of good citizenry. Day after day you see people showing up at the capitol demanding this or that. One becomes hard and thinks everything in politics is done for money, but there actually are a few good people who just do good things for their state and country."

The reason James had become a colonel on the governor's staff was because a lady who was the governor's secretary told him she heard he had a sailboat and she had always wanted to go sailing. James invited her and two of her lady friends for a cocktail sail. She was so excited. The next Tuesday after the sail, she called and asked James to meet her in the governor's office at the same place she had met him before.

When he got there, she said, "I asked the governor to make you a captain on his staff, but we only have colonels."

He was now a colonel on the governor's staff, which meant nothing. James framed his certificate and placed it on his office wall. He laughed every time he looked at it. This certificate made James realize that he was in a different world than the average citizen. If James had been the man who had put up all the signs, he wouldn't have been the good citizen that this man was. James would've likely had a list of the things he wanted from the governor.

"Thank goodness for good citizens," James said.

PARTY TIME, SINGING "THE GOOD OLE BOYS AND ASSOCIATES"

James was an excellent piano player. Sometimes he would entertain at parties. At a friend's party, he announced that he had written a song and he would like to play it for the group.

"The name of the song is 'The Good Ole Boys and Associates,'" James announced. Everyone gathered around the piano, and James started playing. Kimberly had an excellent voice and sang along with James as he played.

We are the Good Ole Boys and Associates
Down at your capitol
We show the senators how to vote
You can count on us
We promote good government every day
That is good government for our clients and friends
We gift them, we charm them, we feed them
Whenever we can
We are the Good Ole Boys
That is
The Good Ole Boys who tell your legislators how
to vote
We wine them and dine them
We care for their families and friends
Who cares?
The Good Ole Boys care
We are the Good Ole Boys, not the best ole boys
That is
The Ole Boys who tell them how to vote
With a smile and handshake
You can depend on the Good Ole Boys
That is
The boys who tell them how to vote
We promise you and we promise them
The best government we can buy
We make certain

Your legislature is happy
That is
When they are voting our way
We are the Good Ole Boys
That is
The Good Ole Boys for good government
Just Good Ole Boys for good government
Everyone sing along!

Many people invited James and Kimberly to parties for the entertainment. Their performance made a party special. Guests especially enjoyed the sing-alongs. They certainly had become the drawing card for political events. They were in high demand on the party circuit.

CHAPTER 13

THE NEW, THE UNREASONABLE, AND THE DISLOYAL

PROPANE HAS A WOLF AT THE DOOR

While sitting in a legislative committee hearing, James noticed that a bill related to the independent propane retailers was being heard, but there seemed to be no one representing the propane companies. The author of the bill wanted to regulate the price of propane. She claimed that propane dealers were overcharging the public and that many people were cold in their homes because they could not afford the gas.

She cried out to the committee, "People are dying. We must do something about this. The trucks are potential fireball bombs traveling our streets and highways. They need to pay a higher fee than other trucks and only be allowed to travel at night or during low traffic periods."

At the close of the meeting, James called a local independent propane retailer and asked him who was representing the industry.

"No one," he replied.

After telling the retailer who he was, he asked if he could meet with him about organizing a lobbying group.

His response to James was, "You damn right we can meet. The public thinks all we are is a bunch of damn dangerous trucks, crowding the goddamn roads and slowing the traffic." Surprisingly, the man who made that remark turned out to be one of the most sophisticated and intelligent men James had ever met.

Although he was never involved in politics as far as running for office or campaigning, he was one of the best James had ever encountered when it came to understanding politics. He taught James a lot about happenings in the world of politics over the next few years.

During their meeting, he told James that several people had tried to organize the independent propane retailers with no success. He pointed out that one person, who later became a state senator, had called a meeting inviting the entire statewide industry to a local hotel to discuss the formation of a lobbying group. He provided a steak dinner for everyone.

While telling him the story, the independent propane retailer told James that everything went well until one guy in the audience stood and said, "I will be happy to join the new group and hire this man as a lobbyist if we don't let that son of a bitch sitting across the room join the group." He pointed to the man and called his name. "That man is the lowlife who lowered the price of gas, started a price war, and caused us all to lose a great deal of money." The "son of a bitch" across the room stood up, stepped up on his chair, and then onto the tabletop. From the tabletop he proceeded to run across four rows of tables to punch the guy in the face. He jumped from the top of the table onto the man who had called him a son of a bitch, wrestling him to the floor and repeatedly hitting him in the face. As a result, the entire room broke out into a fight that caused major damage to the hotel and ended in no possibility of organizing the dealers.

The propane retailer provided James with a list of the major companies in different sections of the state and suggested that James make appointments to visit with each of them. During the next two weeks, James traveled to all sections of the state, meeting with several mom-and-pop propane retailers and a few large independent propane retailers. All of them seemed suspicious of James.

The first meeting was in the largest city in the state. When James arrived at his office, the propane retailer suggested lunch at the country club where he was a member. They rode in his Mercedes-Benz to the club. He questioned James in every way possible to make sure he wasn't sent by one of his competitors. He wanted his company attorney to attend all meetings but didn't explain why. He encouraged James to continue and offered his support.

James met with another independent propane retailer in another city. He, too, was extremely suspicious of James. He asked James what he knew about propane gas, and James's response was, "Nothing."

"Well, I'm the biggest propane retailer in the city and I was a damn plumber, and I still don't know much about propane."

After this visit James continued to the northern part of the state, where he met the smartest man he had ever met in politics, before and after. He was a propane producer and the owner of storage room complexes in multiple cities. He had an extensive understanding of politics. His family was very political, and they had trained him well. He had also been elected to a public office years before and considered running for governor.

Then James traveled west to other cities. No one in the western cities impressed James. They all seemed like a bunch of losers with little or no understanding of politics. After insulting every race except whites, one asked him if he could pass a bill to stop minorities from owning propane companies. In the next city, it was a different story. One of the richest families in the city owned the propane company, a large hotel, and thousands of acres of land. The young man who had inherited the business knew what he was doing. His family was extremely powerful politically. This group of independent propane dealers was a gold mine of political power, but unorganized.

All agreed they needed a lobbyist and that the GOB and Associates would be a good firm to hire. Knowing what happened to the first man who tried to organize the propane industry, James called a meeting of a small group. This was a selective group of leaders who were not likely to get into a fistfight. James and Mike were prepared to buy each of them dinner at one of the city's most expensive restaurants. They discussed the possibilities of forming a lobbying group to pay the GOB. At the end of the meeting and dinner, James gave the waiter his GOB credit card.

The waiter immediately returned it to James and said, "The bill was paid by one of the men when he walked in the door." The dinner, wine, and other drinks had cost more than three thousand dollars and it had been a feast. Others were complaining that they didn't get to pay for the dinner.

At this point James and Mike knew they wanted to represent the propane retailers because they did not mind spending money, and they had a lot of it to spend.

Organizing this group helped make Mike and James an even more significant player in statewide politics. Although few of these men had a higher education, they were one of the smartest groups of people James had ever known. He admired their down-to-earth, straightforward business savvy.

They paid GOB and Associates Incorporated extremely well because they allowed the GOB to keep all the money they could collect from the group and allowed them to use their names on invoices. The GOB simply sent a bill labeled "Lobbying Services" and a letter explaining the amount charged to all propane dealers and collected $100,000 within a month of the invoicing.

In an effort to work with the author of the bill, James and Mike invited the legislator to meet with a small group of propane retailers. They met in Mike's office. One of the propane retailers told James they would rather meet with the author in private. Mike and James waited outside the office for about twenty minutes. The group came out of the office and told the GOB the author was withdrawing the bill. The bill was dead.

After the group left, Mike said to James, "What in the hell went on in there?"

"Maybe we don't need to know," James said.

Mike thought for a minute and said, "You're right."

CRAZY THINGS HAPPEN

Hopefully, the mental health workers James and Mike got to know while working with a group of them did not represent the entire profession.

"As a lobbyist, it's amazing the characters one meets," James said.

"Those who think they want to be a lobbyist should keep in mind that the so-called professional groups are the worst clients," Mike said.

One of the most interesting groups Mike and James ever represented would be a group of professionals, the Mental Health Workers. The lobbyist who represented them had died. They came to the GOB and hired them to pass a bill that would force insurance companies to include their services in health insurance policies. The GOB knew this was basically impossible, but they had the time, and it was worth the gamble. Remember, passing a bill is much more difficult than killing a bill. They gave the GOB a relatively large initial fee and guaranteed them $85,000 if they passed their bill.

The Good Ole Boys represented mostly businesspeople who conducted themselves in a businesslike manner. This group was truly different. They called Mike at home at all hours of the night. The GOB had never received phone calls about lobbying after seven o'clock. Although the group appeared as a united group of professionals, there were religious groups, charitable groups, and others intermingled with them. One or two acted like they were mentally unstable. A few of these people were receiving fees from insurance companies for counseling clients with mental problems, but more and more companies were removing them from the policies. The GOB was unaware of all these factors when they signed the contract.

It surprised everyone when the GOB passed the bill through the house committee and off the house floor. However, when the bill arrived at the senate committee, and the GOB surveyed the committee members, they knew the bill was dead. The vote clearly was not in their favor. The governor had spoken to the chairman of the committee on behalf of the insurance companies and told him to kill the bill. The insurance lobbyists had also worked the committee. Not being a quitter and not wanting to lose the $85,000, the GOB doubled down. They tried to put more pressure on the committee than they had ever seen before, and they did.

One senator called Mike aside and said, "Please, Mike, get these fools off our backs." Mike understood what he was saying but made no attempt to back off. James and Mike wanted to see how much grassroots pressure they could bring to bear. They wanted to beat the governor and the insurance companies.

The night before the bill was to be heard, Mike met with a small group of five or six leaders of the group in a hotel room. They understood they were losing, but there was some slim possibility that they might win. They were lighthearted about the situation and laughed and joked about different scenarios.

"If the senate committee doesn't pass the bill, we could storm them," one female casually said.

Another agreed, "Yes, we should do that."

Mike laughed and thought they were joking.

The next morning, when the bill came up in the senate committee, the room was packed with mental health workers. As expected, the bill failed to pass out of committee.

Then unbelievably, the lady who had suggested charging the committee stood up and screamed at the top of her voice, "Charge!"

Mike and James could not believe their eyes. A group of thirty or more charged the committee as if they were going to drag the senators out of the state capitol and hang each one of them on the capitol steps. The sergeant at arms started threatening anyone who came any closer to any of the senators.

Not believing what they had just seen, Mike and James got up and walked out of the committee room and then out of the state capitol and never contacted another mental health nut again. James and Mike wanted to distance themselves from them as much as possible. The next day they went to each senator's office and apologized for that bunch of stupid sons of bitches they represented.

"We have never represented such a group and never expected what happened," they told the senators.

Unfortunately, the story didn't end there. One of the mental health workers had haunted Mike with daily contact and suggestions that took the story even further. There was no doubt this guy was different. However, he was one of the best educated and had the highest credentials of anyone in the group.

Mike was told that only twenty-five mental health workers in the entire state had the credentials he had.

Realizing the uniqueness of his credentials, he had developed a scheme that was extremely brilliant, but hard to carry out. He continued to call Mike, but Mike would not get involved. He tried to hire James and Mike to help him with his scheme, but they wanted to keep their distance from this group.

He met with a major insurance company and joined forces with it behind the scenes. He wanted a bill passed that would require all mental health workers to work under the supervision of someone with credentials such as his. Almost daily he called and told Mike what was happening. Admittedly, it was interesting to listen as long as the GOB was not associated with him or the group. With the power of the large insurance company, it was just possible that he might pull it off. The insurance company liked it because it could cut the cost of counseling.

The story came to a tragic end. During a disagreement in a local pub, a man shot and killed him. A friend of his was asked to give the eulogy at his funeral. At the funeral, the friend proclaimed him one of the most brilliant politicians he had known and one of the most forward thinking in his profession.

THE JOURNAL

At the morning breakfast meeting, Mike asked James if he was still keeping the journal he was writing.

"Yes, I'll read you what I wrote today. I think you'll find it interesting." James started reading from his journal.

"Lobbying has opened many doors for us and our families. It has introduced us to the world of state legislators, governors, congressmen, and US senators. Many we know on a first-name basis, and we are friends with their family members. We became insiders to the system, a system that is beyond the imagination of most men. We have seen public policy woven into the fabric of society.

"Men who work hard at making the state in which we live a better place became my personal friends. I saw tears roll down a man's face when he had to make a decision that would affect the state far beyond his lifetime. He made this decision with huge groups tugging at him from both sides. He knew that no one truly knew the outcome of his decision. Mike and I have seen men of integrity become victims of character assassination.

"We have seen men vote to protect the public at their political demise. As one of my friends said, 'I'm a lucky man to have experienced this part of life.'

"Then Mike and I saw the other side, the lowlifes of politics. These are men who distorted the facts and conducted opposition research to destroy good people—individuals who would do anything and ignore all basic honorable standards of society to twist the law in their favor. Thank goodness in the legislature and the overall general population of the state, proportionately this was a very small group of people."

James ended the reading.

"That's interesting, and it's very true," Mike said. "Do you remember that young senator who introduced a concurrent resolution to study the cancer problem related to big industry last session?"

"Yes, he's on the Environmental Committee. If I remember correctly, he ran a campaign telling people he would work to clean up the environment."

"Yes, that's him. The bill was deferred. Well, this session someone else introduced the same bill. When the bill came to the vote in the committee this morning, the young senator said he had to abstain from voting because he had a conflict of interest. The chairman of the committee asked him what his conflict was. The young senator said he had just been employed as a lawyer for two industries that would be affected by this bill."

"Damn, they bought him off."

"It certainly appears that way, Mike, doesn't it?"

"When he runs for reelection in a local race for senator, probably nobody will know, because most candidates don't research voting records. Furthermore, his remark about being employed as a lawyer likely would not be found and will not appear in the minutes of the meeting."

"It's all about money, isn't it?"

"It certainly appears that way again and again," James said.

LACK OF LOYALTY HURTS

At coffee one morning in the capitol cafeteria, Mike purchased a newspaper. One of his fellow lobbyists was on the front page. Apparently, the inspector general was investigating her. The newspaper was reporting her huge expenditure of funds on legislators. Alice had hired a travel agency to organize a trip to a beach resort out of the country for all legislators who wanted to go. They simply had to call the travel agent and use a code number provided by Alice and their trip was paid in full.

Alice never expected such a huge turnout. The problem was that Alice had not read the Campaign Financial Disclosure Act, and every ticket she paid for exceeded and violated the reporting requirements. She was charged with

110 violations of the law. The good old utility company she was representing fired her the next day, claiming it had not authorized the expenditure and leaving her with the bill.

"With friends like the utility company, what is a person supposed to do?" Paul said. "We can't trust any of the goddamn clients. They will dump your ass when trouble hits the newspaper." Then he added, "What a group of sons of bitches. You know the expenditure was approved."

All the lobbyists at the coffee table that morning agreed she had been made the scapegoat.

"Why does the goddamn utility company need a lobbyist?" Paul asked. "They should be serving the public. They use our natural resources to produce the power."

"It's a business just like any other business," Donald pointed out.

"I wonder what their issues are," Paul said.

"A big one a few years ago was the permits to build a plant," someone at the table explained.

"They wanted the authorization to sell bonds with the backing of the state treasury," Donald said. "I think the legislature set rates they could charge, but I'm not sure."

"No, those rates are approved by the utility commission, and they gerrymander the districts to make sure they have control of the commission. Their major concern is environmental issues and rights-of-way," someone else said.

"Hell, they're just interested in good government," Smithy said, laughing.

When everyone had stopped laughing, James asked, "Do you think anyone here is interested in good government, other than good government for himself?"

"Damn, James, it didn't take you long to become a pessimist. The system isn't great, but it's better than any other," proclaimed Donald.

"You're right, Donald. God bless America," James replied.

There is an unwritten rule in politics: be careful whom you step on, because they might walk all over you later. Political power is always temporary. One year later, Alice's candidate for governor won. She had given six months of her time traveling the state with him and had contributed thousands of dollars to his campaign. The utility company paid big-time because Alice was appointed by the governor to fill the vacancy of the chairperson of the Utility Commission and had the ear of the governor on many issues.

The utility company offered her large amounts of money to come back to work for it, but she declined and continued to deal out misery to the deserving party. She knew all their dirty little secrets, such as poor citizens paying for big industries' utility bills because they got a massive discount. She had bills introduced to make all customers pay at the same rate, including big industries. She also got the governor to propose state take-over of electrical power, claiming that if the state operated the utility company, then the rates paid by households would be lower. In life and in politics, what goes around comes around.

CHAPTER 14

THING ARE NOT ALWAYS
WHAT THEY SEEM

THE COST OF LABOR

A s lobbyists, Mike and James had never been involved personally in the abortion issue or given it serious thought. Neither had been to church in years. The abortion issue was so emotional that one could not discuss it with close friends. However, a client of Julia, the lobbyist, thought about abortion in a way most people never imagined. Over lunch at the capitol, Julia told the group about a conversation with her client.

"If a person were forced to pick one underlying item for all legislation, it would be the cost of labor," she said. Julia represented a man who was very wealthy and owned a large manufacturing company. She said he would meet with her periodically to discuss legislation.

"We need to get involved in that abortion issue," the client said.

Knowing the client was not highly religious and that abortion had nothing to do with his company—at least Julia didn't think so—what was the angle?

"Why would we want to get involved in that?" Julia asked. "It has nothing to do with your company."

"Oh, yes, it does," he said. "It has a large impact on my company." Using welders as an example, he said, "If government stops abortions there will be more children born. More children means more welders when they grow up. If law allows abortions, there will be fewer births and fewer welders available to work. Fewer welders means my company will receive fewer applications for work and I will have to pay more for welders, or they will go to work for another company. The applicants will want all kinds of benefits. They will join a union and that will be trouble for my company. I must keep the cost of labor down." He continued, "Plus, there will be less people to sell my product to." Then he added, "In business, we must think long term.

"The more welder applications I receive, the more competition there is for the job. This means all they will want is likely enough money to pay their car note and house note, provide food for their family, and buy a six-pack of beer after work each day. They won't care about benefits. They'll say, 'Mr. Boss Man, I just want a job, please.'"

For the company owner, abortion had nothing to do with religion or women's rights or murder or emotions. It was strictly a cost-of-labor matter to him. Unions generally supported a woman's right to an abortion, and the higher the wage, the more dues the union received. More dues meant more political power for the unions.

"At the end of the conversation, the client decided he should not get involved in abortion because it would be traced back to his company, and people would be protesting in front of his manufacturing plant. After that day I started watching every bill to see if I could associate it with the cost of labor, and I rarely found an exception," Julia said.

"Can people really be so hard that they would trade life or death for money?" Mike later asked James.

"It happens routinely in legislatures throughout the country. Remember, Mike, it's sad, but the entire process is all about money and political power."

MEDICAL TECHNOLOGISTS

Mike met a medical technologist in a committee hearing and invited her to lunch at the Greenhouse. He introduced her to senators and representatives who were there. She told them she was there to testify on a bill to create a State Board of Technologists to regulate the profession. The bill had been killed in committee. After lunch she asked Mike what it would cost for them to represent the medical technologists next session.

Mike told her their fees were expensive because, as she could tell from lunch, GOB and Associates Incorporated had very good connections.

"Give me a number," she said.

Remembering how they had been screwed by the occupational therapists, Mike said, "Our minimum fee is eighty thousand dollars for a single-purpose bill."

"Wow. I will pass it by the group. Some of them may want to come to lunch one day. Would that be OK?"

"Certainly, bring them on," James said. "Let us know in advance, and we will make special preparations for you ladies."

Two weeks later the medical technologist called and said she had four technologists from different parts of the state and who would like to come to lunch and meet some of the senators and representatives and talk to the Good Ole Boys. They set the date, and the women appeared for lunch. The legislators talked with them as if they were all friends. Then an unbelievable and spectacular surprise happened. The governor walked in the front door.

He said, "I heard about this operation, and I wanted to see what was going on so near the capitol. I heard I could get a free lunch here."

"Yes, Governor, that's correct. Welcome," Mike said.

After looking around the room, the governor said, "You certainly have some pretty ladies here in the Greenhouse. That is what you call this place, isn't it?"

"Yes, sir, it's referred to as the Greenhouse, and these pretty young ladies are medical technologists," James said. "They are here today asking us to help with a bill to create a State Board of Technologists."

The governor took a seat by one of the prettiest medical technologists, who was from the northern part of the state. He and she were very friendly. The state policeman with the governor took all the women's names and phone numbers so the governor could follow up on the meeting. When he left, he thanked Mike and James for the lunch. He thought they were really doing a service for the legislature, and he told them to keep up the good work.

Later that evening a state policeman called the young lady whom the governor was sitting next to in the Good Ole Boys kitchen. He told her the governor would like to have her as his guest for dinner. If it would be convenient for her to get away from the others, he would send a limo to pick her up.

The next day the technologist who had sat next to the governor called Mike and told him how the governor had taken her to dinner at an out-of-the-way restaurant owned by a close friend of his. She wanted to tell Mike and James how much she appreciated them introducing her to the governor. She also told them that her relationship with the governor might help pass a bill for the technologists. In the same conversation, she asked Mike and James to keep the dinner with the governor confidential. Mike told her they would.

The GOB was so busy they did not have time to deal with another issue. Plus, they thought there was no chance of passage. They subcontracted with Paul to handle the medical technologist. To their great surprise, Paul passed the bill, with the help of the governor. The GOB paid him half of their fee. When he received the $40,000 check, Paul said, "You boys didn't realize how close the girl was to the governor, or you would not have cut this deal with me."

"You're right," James said, laughing out loud.

THE GOB ACCUSED OF CORRUPTION

The GOB learned that when working with a group, the best and the worst behavior of members of the group emerged. During the following event, the very worst behavior emerged.

The president of the Independent Truckers Association asked Mike to come one evening to speak to his group about the legislature. He had called a meeting for the next week. Mike accepted the offer. Truckers were becoming more and more organized. They now had a budget, a CPA, and long-range plans. They didn't know yet that eventually their plans would collapse and the group would dissolve. The days of passing a hat around to collect funds were over.

After the poorly organized business section of the meeting, the president introduced Mike, who made his prepared remarks.

About the time Mike was finishing his talk, a large, rough-looking trucker wearing a white shirt and blue jeans staggered in and walked straight to the front row. Shortly after taking his seat, he stood, interrupted Mike, and started to speak. He tripped over one of the chairs. He was so drunk he could hardly stand.

After regaining his balance, he said, "I came here to tell you that the GOB has cut a deal with the governor to fuck us. They are as crooked as that goddamn governor."

This was a shock to Mike because he had never been accused of being corrupt. He stood before the group speechless.

"Where did you get this information?" asked Mike's friend, Peter.

"I got the information in that barroom across the street just a few minutes ago."

"Was it from a reliable source?"

"Hell, yeah, goddamn it," the trucker said.

Peter immediately came to Mike's defense and told the trucker he needed to go home and change his shirt and put on one without tobacco juice all over the front of it.

"Fuck you," the trucker said. Then he sat down as if nothing had happened. The president adjourned the meeting and apologized to Mike for the disruption and disrespect shown him by the drunken trucker.

Now Mike had a real problem. The trucker had moved and was standing at the exit door of the room, as if he was waiting to grab Mike by the neck and choke him to death. Mike had to pass through that group of rough-and-tumble truckers to get to the door, and he couldn't look like a wimp. So he walked directly to the door where the trucker was standing. He was holding his breath and hoping the trucker wouldn't take a swing at him.

At the door the trucker put his arm around Mike and said, "You really know how to take the shit. You're OK. I like you."

Mike laughed and said, "Thank you," but moved on before the trucker could change his mind. This certainly wasn't a sophisticated group like others the GOB was representing. On his drive home that night, he thought about what the old senator had said: "Politics is a hardball sport." He had never thought about politics becoming physical.

A SMALL BLACK LIMOUSINE

James had been thinking about the limousine and Mr. Dwight. He asked Mike, "You suppose they have a limo in every town for Mr. Dwight?"

"No, they must've rented it at the airport."

"I have an idea," James said. "We should buy a small limo to haul the legislators around."

"That's a great idea!"

"We could pick up any legislator who wanted a ride and drive him wherever he wanted to go. Nan could be the driver."

"Limos cost a lot of money," Mike said.

"No, I saw one just the other day, a used one in good shape for only fifteen thousand dollars. If it doesn't work out, we could resell it."

"I'll talk to the CPA and see what he thinks."

Later that day Mike talked to James after meeting with the CPA and said, "Let's go buy the limo. The CPA said it was a good idea. We can write it all off our taxes, and we're going to need a write-off. We just need to keep a low profile. We don't want to look too flashy. They say if you look like a winner, you will be a winner."

That afternoon Mike and James bought a small black limousine.

Mike couldn't believe how perfectly it had been maintained. "I suppose there's not much of a used car market for limousines," he said.

The inside was immaculate. There was a sunroof, a bar, and a fabulous sound system with controls on both doors in the passenger compartment. In the trunk was a clean, pressed uniform for a driver about the size of Nan. She went to take her test for a chauffeur's license two days later. Then Mike and James told the chairman of each committee that the limousine was available for their use anytime. All they had to do was call Nan to schedule it. At first, it didn't go over well. No one called. Then things changed. Almost every day they were delivering someone somewhere, mostly picking up and taking legislators to and from the airport. Occasionally, legislators would ask to use the limo to take their spouses or friends to dinner. That was no problem. The more they used the limo, the more they were obligated to the Good Ole Boys.

"What's that, Donald?" James asked.

"Many companies will not hire a lobbyist who has worked for a liberal group. At our level—I mean the state level—most liberals do not have the money to pay a lobbyist. Those liberal groups don't understand profit and think we should work for free."

"You're fucking right, and without profit, your lobbying firm is out of business, and you're working as a greeter at Walmart when you're in your sixties," Paul said.

"The same people who hate lobbyists and say things such as it's an awful profession are the same people who have never and will never put up one dime to hire a lobbyist for a good cause," Donald said. "Nor have they ever come before the legislature to testify for a good bill. You guys do realize that less than three percent of America has contributed more than one hundred dollars to a political campaign, much less helped pay for a lobbyist. Most people never put their money where their mouth is, so maybe they get the government they deserve. Hell, the majority of America doesn't even vote."

Kimberly got off the elevator and walked into the coffee shop to pick up a sandwich for lunch. She saw James and Mike at the table with Paul and Donald and waved, but did not speak.

"She is very pretty, and people on the legislative staff say she's a very nice person," Paul said.

"I wonder where she comes from," Donald said. "You know she's connected to somebody politically, or she wouldn't be on the legislative staff."

"You never know who's connected to whom around here, or who is what," James said. "It's a good idea to be nice to everyone." Then James added, "Paul, you're correct—she is really beautiful."

The group moved on to another subject. At that time Paul and Donald did not know that James knew her.

"Paul, did you see the list of lobbyists that was published today by the legislative staff?" Mike asked.

"I haven't seen the list, but I am told there are more than three hundred registered lobbyists on it," Paul responded.

"After working around the legislature for a while I realized there are only about twenty or thirty real lobbyists," Bobby said. "There are people registered as lobbyists who likely couldn't find the front door of the capitol. There are others who appeared occasionally for committee hearings and then went back to their other jobs. One group of vocational educators had a man listed as a lobbyist for their group who owned a one-man advertising agency located in the eastern part of the state. While I was talking to a member of the group, he told me the name of their lobbyist. He had a newsletter that had the lobbyist's picture printed in it. I had never seen this person before that picture. So I asked him for a copy of the newsletter. I showed the picture to several legislators and other lobbyists and asked if they'd ever seen this man. No one had ever seen him in the state capitol. He was a con artist. He had convinced this group that knew little about legislation that he regularly attended the legislative hearings and knew all the important representatives and senators. They were paying this bastard a handsome fee plus expenses while he continued to work at his office on advertising projects for other clients more than one hundred fifty miles away. As far as I could determine, the man had never been to a committee hearing. He was following legislation in the newspaper and by means of a bill-tracking service. What a scam. Sons of bitches like this give us all a bad name."

"Then there are those guys who come to the legislature to attend committee hearings on behalf of groups," James added. "They generally are note takers and have no understanding of the mechanics of politics or the legislature."

"As a full-time lobbyist, this is the guy I wanted on the other side of the issue," Paul said. "He has no idea the votes had already been counted before he testified. Even when he was right, I could beat him every time. Then he would report back to his group that they lost. Of course, he did this on a volunteer basis, so no one would fire him for losing."

Donald, the self-appointed and unofficial senior lobbyist, said, "Most of the three hundred who are registered as lobbyists fit this last description, and that is to our advantage."

The group laughed, and Mike stood and said, "I'm going to get another cup of coffee."

RESOLUTION LOBBYIST—WHAT A GOOD DEAL

A few days later on a cold rainy morning, a large group of ten or more lobbyists gathered in the coffee shop again. The career lobbyists were always manipulating the rules of the legislature. Bobby had come up with a brilliant idea and asked all of them to meet him there to discuss it.

"When a company representative takes a state employee to lunch or dinner, he is lobbying and should have to register as a lobbyist or hire one of us," Bobby said. "Think of how many times such a law would make certain companies need to hire one of us as a resolution lobbyist."

"That's a great idea, Bobby," someone said.

Bobby got a legislator to introduce a bill that required any person taking a state employee to lunch or providing any other form of entertainment to be required to register as a lobbyist. Bobby was encouraging all the others at the table to get behind the bill because it would create multiple new clients.

"Just think," Bobby said. "If all companies regulated by the state that wanted to discuss an issue with a bureaucrat over lunch had to register as a lobbyist, it would be easier to hire one of us than to go through the lobbyist licensing process. All of us would get new clients as a result of such legislation."

"That's brilliant," Donald said. "Let's all get behind it. Just think of all the companies that have to talk to just the environmental boys about fines and regulations, not to mention all the other state agencies."

"Bobby is right," Mike said. "They are lobbying for less regulations or a reduction of a fine when they take them for lunch or dinner."

Eventually, the bill passed unanimously and the governor signed it with no reservations. Every career lobbyist in the capitol worked to make certain the bill passed. After that the lobbying business exploded. The GOB, being established, was able to pick up a number of new clients.

Mike and James brought Paul and Bobby into the GOB as partners and made Josephine a full-time lobbyist. She brought in more than thirty new clients after the governor signed the bill, all because of Bobby's idea. Bobby and Paul brought their clients in with them. Each new client paid the GOB thousands of dollars as a retainer depending on their governmental problems. A second and a third house next to the Greenhouse were purchased and remodeled into office space and painted green. GOB was now the largest lobbying firm in the state. It had five full-time lobbyists and three secretarial staff members. They represented clients ranging from banks, to horse racetracks, finance companies, paycheck loan companies, butane companies, to funeral home owners, to concrete, to medical technologists and a multitude of resolution clients.

CHAPTER 15

LOOKING BACK AND MOVING FORWARD

SESSION SUMMARIZED—FIRM EXPANDS

The president of the senate called the session to a conclusion at midnight on the last day of the session. The GOB had made it through another session of the state legislature as lobbyists. They had done better than they ever dreamed possible. It appeared that the Good Ole Boys were a "good ole team," and it was getting bigger. Their personalities matched as business partners, and their talents varied. James was the public speaker, and Mike was the businessman. Paul and Bobby brought more experience and clients to the firm.

They had just happened upon ideas, such as the Greenhouse, that had made them famous overnight. They were good listeners and learned a lot from other lobbyists who helped them immensely. It had been a whirlwind experience.

"It will take a long time to digest all we have heard and seen. It was nothing like we thought it was going to be," Mike said. "It's not just a bunch of bullshitters bullshitting the bullshitters as we thought. It's a serious business. There are men and women here with great integrity, and there are those who are a disgrace to politics."

"I agree," James said, "but those with integrity certainly outnumber those without it. There are some who can't be bought and others who would do anything for a free lunch. The whole process has changed my thinking about politicians, state employees, and government. The system has its flaws, but overall it works."

"It certainly beats using dueling pistols at sunrise," Mike said.

GOOD CITIZENS OF HAZARDOUS WASTE

When the issue of hazardous waste came up in the legislature, Mike noticed that the polluters were the only ones showing any interest in whether a bill passed or failed. The Sierra Club and other environmental groups would show up, but they were usually college kids who didn't know what they were doing. They had no chance against the lobbyist for the polluters. Other good citizens would show some interest, but none had the political power to overcome the polluters at the state level. The GOB thought there must be a large number of people who dealt with waste who would be interested in abiding by reasonable rules and protecting the environment, not to mention the health of their families.

Bobby and Mike spoke with members of the Sierra Club and asked the group to assist the GOB in organizing such a lobbying group. They readily agreed. They would attend the meeting but would not speak. Such a group speaking at the meeting would scare most hazardous waste operators.

With the Sierra Club on their side, the GOB decided to attempt to organize the good citizens of hazardous waste. They talked to a bureaucrat in the environmental agency and got a list of all companies permitted to handle waste in the state. A cleverly worded letter was developed explaining the need for a political group representing the good guys of hazardous waste. The letter was mailed to several thousand.

Bobby secured a small meeting room at the Holiday Inn. On the date designated for the meeting only about thirty people showed. They all agreed that such an organization was needed and encouraged a second meeting of those showing the most interest.

After the meeting, three people volunteered to help develop the lobbying group. Bobby and Mike took them to lunch to discuss the details. The Sierra Club member accompanied them. During lunch one permit holder asked one of the others, "How did your company dispose of the Agent Orange in fifty-five-gallon drums so cheaply a few years ago?" The questioner said his company had bid on the disposing of it, but they could not do it for anywhere near the price the other company did. The other company's price was half what they could do it for.

"It was simple. We poured the stuff from the fifty-five-gallon drums into one-gallon milk jugs or something of that sort. Then we shipped all the jugs to testing labs all over the United States and asked them to report back to us what was in the jugs. We informed the testing labs that we did not want them to return the leftover product. They could dispose of it, and they did."

"Wow, that was a great idea, and you got away with it! I wish we had thought of that."

The Sierra Club member almost fainted. Then she said, "You did what?" Mike attempted to calm her but couldn't. She then said, "I'm going to report you to the environmental agency." The so-called good citizens of hazardous waste all got up and left the table.

"Can you imagine the UPS drivers not knowing what they were delivering?" the Sierra Club member said. "Thank goodness the federal law has been changed and such jugs have to be marked now or the drivers will not accept them."

Mike and Bobby decided there was no such thing as good citizens of hazardous waste and abandoned the project. At least the ones who represented themselves as good citizens certainly were not.

THE CALL FROM LOUISIANA

"I received an interesting phone call from Louisiana yesterday," Mike told James, Bobby, Josephine, and Paul. "The two guys who called were named Hank and Hebert, and they want to meet with us about helping them develop a lobbying firm in Louisiana. Because of their southern accent it was difficult to understand what they were saying. The one named Hebert pronounced his name 'A-bear.' Hank was from the northern part of Louisiana and Hebert from the southern part. He called it Cajun country. They own and operate a campaign management firm. They managed one campaign for governor and lost, but their candidate came in second. However, they were instrumental in getting the secretary of state elected. They also offer an Institute of Politics to the general public. Hebert designs, prints, and distributes campaign paraphernalia, such as yard signs, billboards, bumper stickers, and placement cards. They want to offer lobbying services, but they have not been able to get any clients. They would like to talk about paying us to help, or they would talk merger of our two firms, if we were interested. Then we could offer campaigning material and educational seminars and have a division that manages races."

"No way do we want to get involved in that state," James said. "Corruption is a way of doing business down there. It has a long history of payoffs, bribes, and patronage that is incomparable to any other state."

"I agree," Bobby said.

"I can tell you guys right now, I don't want anything to do with Louisiana," Paul said. "I know how they treat people from my community down south. Hell, they had the grand dragon of the Ku Klux Klan almost get elected governor in Louisiana. If something goes wrong, I'll get tarred and feathered and you guys will just walk away."

"Times have changed. One-third of the legislators are black down there," Mike said. "You could be very useful in working with the black caucus or helping them select someone from your community to work with them. Remember, we thought our state legislators were corrupt and it was nothing more than a few bad apples in the barrel. How wrong we were. The same may be true in Louisiana."

"I don't think so," said James. "Where there's smoke there's fire, and there is a lot of smoke in the bayou state."

"Well, let's drive down to Louisiana and talk to those guys," Mike suggested. "What do we have to lose? Hell, it would be a break from this place. The trip could be a vacation of sorts for all of us. We could visit the French Quarter."

"OK, but it's going to be hard to convince me to get involved with Louisiana politicians," James said. "You know they had two former governors and one attorney general go to prison. Plus, three insurance commissioners have gone to jail. One insurance commissioner said, 'Everyone elected to the office of insurance commissioner serves two terms in Louisiana, one term as commissioner and one term in prison.' Another governor was committed to a mental institution, got out and was elected to the US Congress. Are you sure you want to get involved with that?" They all laughed out loud.

"I don't know, but I at least want to talk to them," Mike said. "I researched Hank, and I think he has oil money, if I found the right Hank. He told me on the phone they would be willing to make a sizable investment in GOB and Associates Incorporated and would consider a merger of the GOB and their firm."

"OK, call them and set up a meeting," James said, and they all agreed.

HARVARD AND BEYOND

After returning from Italy, James had read about a program at Harvard University pertaining to lobbying. Kimberly encouraged him to attend. It was a one-week intensive program offered by the Harvard Institute of Politics. James discussed it with the GOB, and they agreed with Kimberly that it was a good idea. James applied and was accepted.

"I refuse to attend unless you go with me, Kimberly," James said. "You can shop and see the city while I'm in class."

"Yes, I can shop for things for the wedding. We can also meet some of my Harvard classmates at the Harvard Club. It will be interesting to see how they respond to a 'good ole boy.'"

The seminar proved to be more beneficial to James than he could have ever imagined. He met leaders in politics from throughout the United States. After listening to all the discussions, he realized that the Good Ole Boys had been very lucky. Few lobbying firms had gotten so many good clients in such a short period of time.

While in class, he learned of a weekend seminar on how to get elected to Congress. Kimberly encouraged him to stay over the weekend and take the short course. She told him, "You can never tell—it could be of great value in the future, and besides, we are already here."

The weekend course started at six o'clock in the morning and ended at six o'clock at night. It was intense. The course covered everything from planning the campaign to raising money to the victory party. Conducting opposition research, handling the media, campaigning, working with consultants, and getting out the vote were also covered. Kimberly would quiz James each night as to what he had learned. She seemed so interested that James asked her if she was planning to run for Congress.

She said no, she just liked the subject.

Three of the best campaign managers in the country were introduced and spoke to the class. Professional fund raisers addressed the class as well. A CPA firm that specialized in campaign-finance compliance gave a brief overview of campaign finance laws and the importance of compliance. It was a comprehensive course about an area in which

James had some background from college, but the seminar was more detailed and more practical.

When the seminar was over, Kimberly talked James into staying over three more days so she could show him the city and they could do more shopping together. She told James she had decided she was going to have to quit her job so she would have time to plan the wedding.

"We could just get a local judge to marry us," James said.

"That's not going to happen. I am my parents' only daughter. This is a once-in-a-lifetime event, and it's going to be the society wedding of the year."

"Really!"

"Yes. You just relax and do what you're told, and you will be OK." They both laughed. James was not the kind of guy to do what he was told. But he would listen, because whatever it took to make Kimberly happy, he would do for the rest of his life. He had fallen head over heels in love with her.

James was a hit at the Harvard Club. The group enjoyed hearing him talk about everyday politics at the state level.

"You had them chasing you to hear your stories," Kimberly told James. "If you can charm that group of snobs, you can charm any group. I have never seen them react to anyone like they did to you. Mike's right—you are a natural-born politician."

On the flight home, Kimberly asked, "What did you think about the congressional election course?"

"Well, it made getting elected seem a lot simpler than I thought. You first have to have a base, and then it's a matter of organization and planning."

"You have a base."

"What base?"

"Gravel producers, timber, concrete, funeral home owners, lumber dealers, theater managers—and the list goes on. They all love you. You can deliver great speeches. You have a clean background. I know because Daddy checked on you. Plus, you have the most important base of all, a wonderful wife who will support you in a race for Congress."

"Me, run for Congress?" James asked, surprised.

"Absolutely, yes! You need to start planning now, but after the wedding, of course. We're both going to be very busy getting that together. Plus, James, I know you realize by now that we have more money than we can spend in ten lifetimes. Why not invest some in our country? You're honest, realistic, and good-looking. What else could someone want in a congressman? In addition, if anyone decides to run against you, we can buy him off!"

CHANGED HISTORY

After James returned from Harvard, Mike, Bobby, Josephine, and Paul wanted to know what he had learned. James told them about a speaker who spoke about how lobbyists had influenced the history of the United States. The speaker was one of three people who had been asked by Lyndon Baines Johnson, president of the United States, to determine how to integrate American schools. The speaker said that after they consulted with numerous people and researched the possibilities, the three came up with three suggestions for Johnson. They were:

1. Pass a federal building permit law that would require all new subdivisions to have houses available for people of all income levels. For example, in all neighborhoods, houses would range from $10,000

to $1,000,000 and up. To get a permit, the contractor would have to build $10,000 houses, $20,000 houses, $30,000 houses, and so on until all income levels were included. The group believed that mixing the poor and the rich in all subdivisions would lessen the fear of each other. The claim was that the rich would be more interested in what happened to poor children if they lived next door to them. Also, such integration of subdivisions would eliminate the fear that many have of people who do not look, talk, or act like them.

2. Bus children from one section of town to another to attend school.

3. Subsidize loans on houses when the rich or middle class buy and live in poor neighborhoods.

"After Johnson listened to their proposals, he pulled his chair close to his desk and, with a concerned face, looked straight at the group and said, 'Obviously, the building permit idea is the method you men favor, but we can't beat the construction industry. Their lobbyists are too strong, and they will never allow such a national building permit law to pass out of the house or senate, much less both. Such a bill would be dead upon arrival.

"'The subsidizing method would meet with mixed reviews, and the banks would not take the risk. The banking lobbyists would pick holes in such a bill. The banking lobbyists are even stronger than the construction lobbyists. The education lobbyists will oppose your busing recommendation, but we can beat them. They are weak.'

"At that point American history changed because Johnson supported the busing of children across town for the purpose of integrating schools rather than integrating subdivisions. Without the influence and power of lobbyists, subdivisions would have been integrated, and white flight would not have occurred. The speaker pointed out that America would be a different country today if Johnson could have beaten the construction lobbyists."

"If the people only knew how the system is corrupted by lobbyists!" Mike said. "Before we got into this business, I never imagined that the history of the country could be changed by a group of lobbyists. It's amazing that Johnson was so powerful that he could pass the Civil Rights Act but couldn't beat the construction lobbyists."

"There is a good argument that lobbyists should be banned from the political process," Bobby said.

Mike immediately roared with laughter. "Bobby, are you crazy? All the money we're making? We don't want government to be *that* good!"

They all agreed and had a good laugh.

PERMISSION TO MARRY

Kimberly said, "James, my parents have invited us to their house for dinner next Wednesday night. You know I have accepted your proposal for marriage, but my father hasn't. You may want to talk to him. Don't worry about my mother; she's going to love you."

On Wednesday of the following week, Kimberly and James arrived at her parents' home. It was an elaborate, twenty-room stone-and-granite mansion. Kimberly rang the doorbell. James turned and started for his car in the driveway.

"Where do you think you're going?" Kimberly asked as she pulled him back. "Don't be nervous. They're going to love you."

"I hope you're right," he said.

The butler met them at the door and welcomed James to the family home. Then he led them to the living room, where Kimberly's parents were waiting. They were older, mature, gray-haired, and dignified looking. Kimberly's father, Jim, was about the same height as James. Her mother, Irene, was a very distinguished-looking lady. James could tell that she had been beautiful in her younger years.

After the usual pleasantries, Kimberly's father invited James into his study. In the study, Jim told James that his name was also James but that people called him Jim. Then Jim said, "Kimberly said you have some business you would like to discuss with me tonight."

"Yes, sir, I do. I would like to ask your permission to marry your daughter."

"Will you love her and be good to her?"

"I will."

"You know she is my only daughter, and I'm very protective of her."

"Yes, sir, I realize that."

"Permission granted," Jim said. The permission was granted like Eisenhower granting permission to invade Normandy. "I welcome you into the family. Now, young man, you do realize there are some heavy responsibilities that come with marrying into this family." At that point James had no idea how heavy the responsibilities would become or how his life would change forever. He would learn that marrying a woman with money comes with challenges he would never expect.

"I've never seem Kimberly happier," Jim said. "What is the date of the proposed wedding?"

"I don't know. Kimberly hasn't told me yet."

They both laughed, and Jim said, "You keep that attitude, and you will be married for a long, long time. Kimberly's mother sends me in the direction I need to go, and I always appear to be agreeable whether I am or not. Kimberly told me you spent some time at Harvard this year."

"Yes, sir, I took some courses in political planning and strategy."

"Politics is interesting," Jim said. "It's good that you are learning how to manage the politicos. That will become very useful in life. No matter whether you like them or not, they are a force to be dealt with. Usually they are easily controlled," Jim continued. "In a chess game, the politicians are the pawns. There are some who are more like a rook, meaning they are fairly straightforward but not nearly as powerful as a bishop. The tycoons of industry and business are the kings and queens. Some politicians are so devious that you have to think of them as the knights. They are the most dangerous of all because you never know whether they are going to go to the left or right or up or down. Did they teach you that at Harvard, son?"

"No, sir, I have never heard anyone compare politicians to chess pieces."

The butler came to the door and said, "Dinner is served."

"Come on, James; let's join the ladies."

Dinner was light: salad, Chilean sea bass, roasted root vegetables, and a pear tart for dessert prepared by the kitchen staff. Kimberly's mother asked where they had met. Before James could say the broom closet, Kimberly spoke quickly and said, "At work."

Kimberly's father looked at Irene and said, "James has asked permission to marry Kimberly."

"And did you approve?"

"Yes. Do you?"

"Absolutely, yes!" Irene said excitedly. "Well, it appears we have a wedding to plan!"

Kimberly held her left arm out with her hand dangling to show off the plastic engagement ring. Jim said, "That looks like the one I gave you, Irene."

"Almost. The one you gave me was made of wood. You carved it from a tree branch. It's in my jewelry drawer, and it is still the prettiest ring you ever gave me." James remembered that was almost exactly what Kimberly said when he gave her the plastic ring. Irene then said, "The wedding ring was nothing more than a simple gold band. But he promised to replace it with something better when he made his first million, and he did. Knowing how frugal Jim is, I never expected it to be so nice." She held her left hand out, showing James her large diamond.

"Jim, you have set high standards for me," James said. But James did not know that Irene was going to give her mother's diamond ring to him to give to Kimberly before the wedding.

"Have you set a date and made any wedding plans?" Irene asked.

"No," Kimberly said. "We wanted your approval first."

"I hope you will let me help," Irene said.

"Certainly, Mother."

"Are you going to hire a wedding planner?" Irene asked.

"No. I'm sure you and I will be able to handle it."

"That's good. Being frugal is important," Jim said.

After dinner they went to the family room for after-dinner cocktails, but on the way, Kimberly and her father wandered off to Jim's office. Jim asked Kimberly if she was sure about James.

"Yes, Father. He is not marrying me for money. James thought I was a civil servant and living on a state salary for a long time before I introduced him to any of our family's holdings. He is honest, trustworthy, and he loves me. Furthermore, I learned from you to never make an important decision based on emotions. I love him very much, but I have also looked at the positive and negative characteristics of the man I will marry, as you always told me to do. Like most men he needs a little sophistication, but I'm working on that. He's a fast learner. I didn't tell him anything about our family business or properties until I knew him well and knew that he had fallen in love with me. A woman can tell. He is the man I have been looking for all my life. Until last week, James had no idea as to the size of our fortune."

"You sound like your mother," her father said. "I know she loves me, but she has such an analytical mind. Sometimes I think she married me so she could have someone help her manage her money. I just hope our tremendous family fortune doesn't scare him away."

"Don't worry, it won't."

"As you know, your mother kept me in the dark as to her family's fortune," Jim said. "It sounds as if you have handled it well. It's interesting to see family history repeat itself right before my eyes. I am so happy for you and expect some wonderful grandchildren soon." They both laughed as they joined Irene and James in the family room by the fireplace.

In the family room, Irene asked, "Would you consider getting married in April, the month your father and I got married? That's a wonderful time of year to get married. The season is changing, and the weather is nice almost world-wide. The rain is light and the spring flowers are starting to bloom."

"Yes, Mother, that's a wonderful idea," Kimberly said, and James agreed.

THE SAFE HOUSE

Kimberly continued opening up to James about her finances. She told James that she had another house near her mother and father. She referred to it as the safe house. She bought the condo because it was near the state capitol and easy to get to work. It was also easy to secure.

"Would you like to have lunch Saturday at my house and spend the weekend with me?" she asked.

"Yes, of course. What is your address so I can put it in my GPS." She said her street was not on the city map, so it was not locatable on a GPS. James asked her if she was sure.

"My father had my street removed from the city maps for my protection."

Her street was more like a private drive. She had bought the street from the city. When Kimberly built the house, she also bought all the neighbors' homes and tore them down and beautifully landscaped each side of the street. From the guardhouse to Kimberly's front door was about two blocks. A private gate with a call box was placed at the entrance to the street. A stone wall was built around the entire property. When Kimberly was at home, Jack lived in the guardhouse. In addition to Jack's being there, the property was monitored 24-7 by a private guard service that worked only for Kimberly's father. Kimberly's mail was delivered to Jack's home so that no one could get her mailing address and find her house.

The next day, Saturday, James arrived at Kimberly's home at noon. He was absolutely shocked when he saw her house. It was made of marble and granite and was located in an old section of town where the captains of industry lived.

"I'm impressed!" he said. "You can certainly keep a secret."

Kimberly showed James around the house and described the construction details. The tour ended in her bedroom, where they passionately made love. After making love, James entered her bathroom, which was three times the size of his apartment. There was plumbing equipment James had never seen before. The tub was huge, and the shower was bigger. There was a steam bath, a sauna, and a massage table. They spent the rest of Saturday and all of Sunday just hanging out, except when they were working out in her gym.

"Do you think I should invite Mike and Catherine to this house or the condo?" Kimberly asked James.

"That's your decision to make," James answered. "It doesn't matter to me. It will be interesting to see their reactions."

One week later, Kimberly invited Mike and Catherine to her home for dinner. James gave Mike detailed directions to get to the house. He explained that at the guardhouse, he would have to identify himself with a picture ID to be allowed entrance. As planned, Mike and Catherine arrived at the house. Mr. Lane, the family butler, met them at the door in his usual black tie.

Catherine, stunned by the house, said, "This is a magnificent house. Is this Kimberly's family home?"

"No, it's just Kimberly's," James said. "She will be down in a minute."

Mr. Lane announced, "We are serving Grey Goose martinis, up, shaken, dirty, and two olives, with or without anchovies."

Mike and James requested anchovies, and Catherine wanted "without."

Kimberly came down from upstairs and requested one without anchovies. She asked Mr. Lane what he was serving for dinner.

"The cook has prepared arugula salad with oranges and caramelized fennel, grilled salmon, potato and porcini gratin, broccoli with a lemon caper sauce, and a chocolate praline tart."

"That sounds delicious," Kimberly and Catherine both said.

"This is a fabulous house, Kimberly," Mike said. "I'm amazed how you have managed on a state employee salary."

"Yes, Mike, I do well on the underpaid state employee salary." Kimberly knew Mike was fishing for information on her financial situation, but she didn't bite the hook. As she had always done with James, she avoided discussing any of her background. She laughed and said, "I'll teach you how to make money in politics someday."

To change the subject, Kimberly asked, "Did James tell you we are getting married?"

"Yes, congratulations!" Catherine said.

The dinner continued with the usual small talk. After dinner Mr. Lane informed the group he was going home and asked if anything else was needed. Mike and Catherine thanked him for the delicious meal and his service. Kimberly walked him to the door.

At the door and beyond hearing range of the others, Mr. Lane asked in a protective manner, "Does your father know you're getting married?"

"Yes, and he has granted James permission to marry me. As a matter of fact, mother and father are very excited. I'm surprised they haven't told you."

"I have been out of town on vacation during the past month."

"My father has already requested grandchildren." They both laughed.

The next day James asked Kimberly about the background check Jack ran on Mike.

"Yes. That is routine. Background checks are run on everyone who gets close to the family."

"What were the results?"

"I think Jack indicated you and he were escaped convicts. We will talk about that later." She laughed and said, "No, there was nothing bad in the report. I'll show it to you."

Kimberly later asked James to be sure to remind Mike to keep her house and other information about her confidential.

James said he would.

"It was a wonderful night, and Mike and Catherine are lovely people. I hope they become lifetime friends," Kimberly said.

THE WEDDING

James and Kimberly's wedding was the social event of the year in the capital city. An invitation was a highly prized item. Kimberly chartered an airplane and paid the expenses for her friends from Paris and New York to attend the wedding. More than five hundred people attended. The cost was outrageous, but Kimberly's family spared no expense. They honeymooned in Santorini. The honeymoon was wonderful. They stopped by Paris on the way back to the States.

THE RACE FOR THE SENATE

After the wedding, when things had calmed down, Kimberly brought up the idea again of James's running for the US Congress. On several occasions prior to this discussion, Kimberly and James had pondered the subject. She pointed out to James that he would make an excellent statewide candidate because of his good looks, his ability to deliver a mesmerizing speech, his understanding of politics, and his friends who would help with name recognition in the business world throughout the state.

"With all the groups that Bobby and Paul have represented, they will be a big help to you also," she said. "I'm certain they will get on the campaign trail with you. And working with the GOB has given you an understanding of how the system works. You know, some are going to say you don't have enough experience in politics to run for office. But they are wrong. It's like going to college. If you run for class president the first year, no one knows your faults. If you wait until the second year, they have begun to find things wrong with you. By the fourth year you are dead meat because familiarity breeds contempt. So now is the time to run. You will be the underdog, and that will catch them off guard."

James thought about it for a few minutes and in a favorable tone agreed. "Running could be a good idea, and if I'm going to run, this is the time to do it."

"You're right, James. Now is the time, because you have a huge group on both sides that likes you, and the liberals don't have a strong candidate. You will have to run as a conservative; I know deep down inside you are almost a liberal, but the public doesn't know that. If you stay on the talking points, no one will ever know your real position. Thank goodness you don't have a voting record for them to browse through. It's difficult to criticize someone who doesn't have a voting record." Kimberly was extremely good at making James think things were his idea. She was a better political strategist than James, but he didn't know it yet.

"Senator Joe is retiring but has not announced it yet," Kimberly inserted as an informational point.

"Yes, I hear he's looking for a lobbying job," James said.

"We can get him to support you. You would be a shoo-in to take his place if he endorses you, and I have no doubt he will. The polls show he still controls thirty-five percent of the vote. He owes us, plus Daddy can get him a lucrative DC lobbying contract. A member of the house usually gets a one-million-dollar signing bonus plus stock options when he retires and goes to work for a Fortune 500. You know, he's not retiring because he wants to give up his seat. He's retiring because the polls show he can't win reelection, but his thirty-five percent of the vote makes him a force not to be ignored. He can sway an election one way or the other. He needs a job, and we can provide him very good employment. We don't have to worry about his cooperation. He always goes where the money is, and guess what, James? We have the money." They both laughed.

"Our conservative governor could call a special election quickly after Senator Joe announces his retirement," James said, "and the senator will let us determine his retirement announcement date. The election could be just forty-five days after he makes his retirement public."

"You're right, James. Senator Joe and the governor will work with us, especially after they hear that we plan to spend a minimum of fifteen million dollars."

"We need to get the word out that we're going to spend at least fifteen million if I run for the Senate, because that will scare a lot of candidates away. Who in his right mind would want to take on a war chest like that?"

"With a war chest like that, we could elect a jackass to the Senate," Kimberly said.

"Kimberly, are you comparing me to a jackass?"

"No, James, you would never be a jackass. You're the most wonderful man, and I am so lucky to have married you. I love you so much."

James laughed. "Thank you, Kimberly. I love you, too. Because we will know when the governor plans to call the special election, we could have our TV time locked and yard signs and bumper stickers ready to go. The opposition will not know the dates in advance and will be caught off guard. That will give us a tremendous advantage."

"You're right, James. It's like my daddy says: 'Politics is like a horse race. The first one out of the gate is more likely to win, if he maintains a steady pace.' We can buy all the premier TV time, leaving the opposition with nothing to buy except second-rate programs. We can hire the campaign manager who has the best track record in the country to manage your campaign. Such a person would be expensive, but we can afford it."

"Hell, Kimberly, the one with the best record is a campaign manager for the liberal side."

"You're talking about Eddie D. He doesn't care about your party or your beliefs. He's just in it for the money. If he can't help, he'll recommend someone with his abilities who can. I know him from the Clinton and the Bush campaigns. He was always coming around for money. Plus, Bill or Hillary will also help. Daddy spent the night in the White House several times under both the Bush and Clinton administrations."

"But Kimberly, the last thing we need the public to know is that someone in our family had any association with Hillary. I'm sure the majority of voters in the state don't like her."

"I'm not so sure of that. Women love her," Kimberly said. "It will be a nasty campaign, James. The opposition researcher will find and broadcast every bill you and Mike lobbied for. People will think you broke every car windshield that has ever been broken in the state. You lobbied for the damn gravel trucks, and everyone hates those trucks. I can see the ad now. Imagine a gravel truck dropping rocks all over the road, causing crashes and breaking windshields. The ad would show you driving, and the signs on the truck would read 'Vote for Me.' For God's sake, a poll taken last week showed that the large majority of people in our state hate gravel trucks. Have you ever been in a gravel truck?" Before James could say no, she said, "You will be the cartoon character for gravel trucks for certain, but we can overcome it. Money talks.

"You have not lobbied for anything so bad that a good ad can't reverse. You just simply say that you want to keep government out of business. People will be surprised to see how many folks on the liberal side will vote for keeping government out of the way of business. They do this because they work for business, and when government restricts business, it takes money out of the worker's pocket. You remember how the unions joined with you and Mike when government restrictions on concrete trucks had the potential of lowering workers' wages and eliminating union truck drivers?"

"Yes, I remember. Everyone votes his pocketbook."

"Brown Timber Company would damn sure help," she said. "He's tied with the governor and certainly could get the governor to shorten the election period. All those people who were given football tickets and were flown to games in Brown Timber's airplanes will be behind you for sure.

"We will need to put together a campaign committee in each district and city of the state. We can ask a concrete producer, a timber man, a theater guy, and others from groups represented by the GOB to serve on these committees. Paul and Bobby can get someone from each of the groups they represent. Bobby can bring the bankers aboard. I think Paul has some connection to the courthouse crowd and can bring many of them to our side."

"If I get elected to the Senate, do you think the president will take us flying on Air Force One with him?"

"He better fly both of us on Air Force One and land in the state at least two or three times during the campaign to show his support for you. My father helped put him in office, and he will help take him out if he doesn't."

She thought for a minute and said, "You can certainly get the gay vote because of all the little theater managers. The bill you and Mike passed for them provided more money for their theaters than they could imagine. Certainly they will turn out the vote for you. They all have families in addition to gay partners. Their group is much bigger than people imagine. James, you have developed one hell of a base. Because of the GOB, your name is like Coca-Cola among the business community."

"You're right. During the years we've been in business, we have certainly been involved with a large number of people in the business community. I met many of them in the State Business Association meetings and the Monday sessions with the Fortune 500 lobbyists, and they trust me. All the pro-business speeches I gave before business associations made me a fixture on the business lecture circuit."

"This is what's going to get you elected—the conservative business community. Just wait and see, Senator James."

"I like that word, *senator*," James said.

"I will have a pollster do some research to see who and what the challenges might be," James continued.

Then James moved on to another subject. "I really enjoy Paris," he said. "The city is so busy. I just wish they would quit blowing their goddamn horns. I've never heard anything like it."

"No, that is just part of the charm of the city. Blowing the horn is as French as the Louvre. It's a part of their culture."

James called Eddie D., the liberal pollster and campaign manager. His fees were outrageous. Kimberly told Eddie D. they would commit to fifteen million dollars for the race, but he had to raise the rest. Eddie D. said they should consult a campaign finance specialist to make certain they didn't violate the Campaign Financial Disclosure Act.

"It will take about two weeks to complete the polling," Eddie D. said. "We must design the questions to produce a correct assessment. Then we must put together a focus group and a door-to-door random sample by canvasing selected homes and neighborhoods in the state. All economic levels and classes of people in the state must be in the sample. We especially must look at those who voted in previous congressional races. Due to the Medicare issues that are in the news, we will survey a large number of those over sixty-five. In the end, we will know what your possibilities of being elected are."

Although James's name recognition in the business community was extremely good, the general public didn't know him. The only thing helpful to him in the public was that when he asked if they would vote for a business lobbyist, the conservatives in all surveying methods overwhelmingly answered yes. It was to James's advantage that the word *lobbyist* was not a dirty word to people in the state, at least among those who were likely to vote and contribute to a campaign in the bellwether precincts.

As a result of the poll, James decided to run. It was clear that there was some possibility he could get elected.

"New blood is needed in the Senate," James said, "and I believe I can fill those shoes."

THE ANNOUNCEMENT

James told Mike, Josephine, Paul, and Bobby about his plans to run for the US Senate at their breakfast meeting. At first they did not believe him. He had never held public office, but they soon realized he was serious. He told them about the polling data and the money that was going to be spent. To avoid conflicts with clients, he was going to take a leave of absence.

"You don't need to take a leave," Bobby said. "Our clients would love to have one of us in the US Senate. As a matter of fact, I'm going to get on the phone today and start organizing supporters from our client list."

"Me, too," Paul added.

"I must admit this surprises me, but I think you are going to make a great US senator. Having one of the good ole boys in the Senate will do nothing but make us a more powerful lobbying group," Mike said cheerfully.

Mike, Paul, Josephine, and Bobby each took on a major responsibility in the campaign. They worked for James from five o'clock in the morning to midnight, stopping only to take care of a client's problem.

Sam's hotel gave James several rooms to use as campaign headquarters and provided daily refreshments and food for campaign workers. Old Senator Jackson called in some favors. Smithy's pharmaceutical firm made large contributions to James's campaign. Alice put the governor's campaign machine to work for James. Josephine coordinated the statewide campaign offices with remarkable efficiency. Nan became James's driver, without her chauffeur's uniform, of course. The state Manufacturing Association endorsed James, and the unions didn't launch an all-out campaign against him. They knew that they could work with him behind the scenes. Lobbyists that James didn't know endorsed him. They wanted to see one of their own get elected.

The trip to Louisiana had to be put on hold for a while—at least until after the campaign. Mike told Hebert and Hank about James running for the Senate and that they would have to delay their trip. They said they would send a contribution to help him. The next day by express mail James received a check for $25,000 made out to his campaign. It was his first large contribution.

Who to hire as a campaign manager was the priority the next day. "Everyone has a male campaign manager," James said. "If we hire a woman campaign manager, this could get the female vote. We need to poll that issue because it can go both ways. Some of the conservatives won't rally behind many female issues."

A poll was conducted overnight, and the result was a statistical tie.

Then the question was put before a focus group; the results were more toward hiring the female, but not by much. When the question was reworded, James did pick up a few votes but also lost a few. It was a toss-up, so James decided to remain with the traditional male campaign manager. Kimberly agreed. It was too high a risk, and the pollster argued that you never knew what the opposition would do with it. Such a brave hiring gamble could be twisted in many directions. Later they decided to add a female as comanager, and that worked out well.

It was going to be difficult for the opposition to run an ad. The best-known political columnist wrote a critical column about James's massive buying of radio and television time. Overnight, a yard sign crew covered the entire state with more than fifty thousand signs along the sides of roads and in supporters' yards. Billboards appeared as if they had been dropped from the sky during the night. The liberals jumped on this and promoted the idea that James was a rich man trying to buy his way into the US Senate. James countered by saying he was not a rich man; he was an employee of a small business until he hit it lucky in the stock market. He grew up middle class and understood how difficult it was for families to put food on the table and have health insurance. He had operated a small business and understood the struggle to make a payroll and pay taxes.

Another ad said James was out of touch with the common man and showed him at a polo match and playing tennis at a country club. One ad featured James's sailboat. That ad showed two blue-collar guys in a small fishing boat looking at the sailboat and referring to it as a "blow boat." The ads were hitting home. James was dropping in the polls. Then James countered with pictures of him welding and cutting wood on a table saw. These ads touched base with the common man. It was as if they thought, *What if he is an elitist? He knows how to do things with his hands. He's one of us.*

The seminar James had attended at Harvard was backfiring. The opposition was running ads calling him a Harvard man and trying to show him as an elitist. The ads never mentioned that James had only attended a seminar at Harvard. They made him look like he had received a four-year degree.

The theme of one radio ad against James played on a country-western station and was aimed at the less-educated voter. It went like this: "We don't need any of them there rich Harvard boys here." A bumper sticker read, "Vote NO Harvard Guy. Vote #6." James put the ads to sleep with an expensive infomercial aired just prior to the election. He described himself as coming from the working class and discredited the campaign to make him appear elitist. The ad also featured James's former boss and others describing him as a hardworking, down-to-earth person who the state needed to send to the US Senate. Kimberly's Harvard connection paid off. Money from Harvard grads rolled into campaign headquarters to support James in his race.

The president came through and landed Air Force One in the state three times. The vice president landed Air Force Two twice. Each time, James was pictured greeting them on the ground or walking off Air Force One or Two with them. Each landing site was carefully selected, with the planes landing in cities where James's poll numbers were low. Kimberly described the pictures as "killer ads." This made James look like a man who could handle the Senate. It showed him as a man with important connections that could help bring home the bacon to the state. The campaign managers bragged correctly, "Never in state politics has there been so much presidential attention given to a candidate for the US Senate."

There is always the October surprise in a campaign. This means the opposition holds its biggest negative ad until just days before voting takes place so that it will be on the minds of the voters on Election Day. James's campaign staff was waiting, but it never happened. It was clear the opposition had run out of money. An October surprise was their only chance of beating James, and it had fizzled. There is an old saying in politics: "Money is the mother's milk of politics," and they had run out of milk.

The October surprise was happening to the opposition. One of James's ads was devastating. Before James ran the ad, he talked to the opposition candidate and told him what was going to be in the ad and offered him the opportunity to drop out of the race.

The opposition candidate told James, "Go to hell. I'm not dropping out." James told him he was already down in the polls. This ad would hurt his reputation as a man, and he would prefer not to run it. The opposition candidate repeated, "Go to hell" and walked away from James.

The ad showed a document found in the public record. It was only a piece of paper, but in the TV ad, it was devastating. The paper was a certified copy of a delinquent property tax notice. Actually, the opposition candidate missed the payment by one week and paid the penalty. However, James's ad did not make mention of that. It made the opposition candidate look like a man who wanted to go to the Senate to tax others when he didn't pay his own. The last-minute ad did not give the opposition time to respond. Plus, any response would be on the defensive.

Another ad that truly helped James with the women's vote was his ex-wife's ad. The opposition had spread rumors that James was a divorcee and had many problems with his ex-wife. Sarah, his ex-wife, and Kimberly had become good friends, and she volunteered to hold events in her home and attend fund raisers for James. Sarah walked door to door with Kimberly, asking people to vote for James. TV cameras followed them and made a positive story out of the two wives campaigning together for James. Sarah explained to everyone that she was the ex-wife and that she was voting for James.

In a radio ad Sarah and Kimberly made together, Sarah said, "I am James's ex-wife, and I'm voting for him. James is an honest man, and we need him in the Senate."

Then Kimberly said, "I am his present and last wife, and I am voting for him, too."

Then both said simultaneously, "We are both voting for him because he will make a great senator." This was another killer ad. This put all rumors to sleep.

The race was over. The votes had not been counted, but it was obvious what the outcome was going to be. Two days later, James and Kimberly were in a hotel suite in Sam's hotel with Kimberly's mother and father and James's mother. James's father had died years before. Mike and Catherine were there, as well as the campaign manager and several friends, including old Senator Jackson, Peter, Smithy, Bobby, Sam, Josephine, Brian, and Paul. Even Donald was there, because James wanted everyone in politics to know he did not desert people who helped put him in office, no matter who they were. They were all watching the election returns.

First the urban votes were reported, and James was losing significantly. After about an hour, the suburban votes started rolling across the TV screen. James won by a landslide. The champagne was flowing. James and Kimberly and all the others in the room went down to the ballroom to thank the voters.

On James's way down to face the TV cameras and make his acceptance speech, Kimberly whispered softly into his ear, "You could be president."

The elevator door opened, and Kimberly and James stepped to the side to talk. "The campaign starts in a few minutes," Kimberly said. "Speak presidential! Talk about foreign affairs, national defense, health care, and so on."

"Kimberly, do you want to be the first lady?"

"Well, that could be interesting. What else do we have to do?"

James walked to the grand ballroom stage where the crowd was screaming and hollering in support. The GOB started hollering in unison, "James for president, James for president," and the crowd tuned in.

(To be continued)

ABOUT THE AUTHOR

For more than a decade Dr. Murphy was the owner and manager of a lobbying firm he created after working in state government as a high official for seven years. Later he served as a legislative assistant to a state senator.

He worked in three campaigns for governor. He was a major advisor and served on the campaign management team for a United States Congressman running for governor. That candidate came in second out of sixteen contenders.

Dr. Murphy earned his doctor of education degree from the University of Arkansas. He owned and organized a school that specialized in law related subjects for more than twenty years. He and his wife divide their time between Louisiana's capital city, the New Orleans French Quarter and the city of Guanajuato, Mexico..